SPECTRUM®

Math

Grade 7

Published by Spectrum®
an imprint of Carson-Dellosa Publishing
Greensboro, NC

Spectrum®
An imprint of Carson-Dellosa Publishing LLC
P.O. Box 35665
Greensboro, NC 27425 USA

ISBN 978-1-4838-0875-8

07-152177811

Table of Contents Grade 7

Table of Contents, continued

Geometry - Circles - Formula

$C = D \times pi$

$C = 2 \times R \times pi$

$A = pi \times R^2$

Parts of a Circle:

$pi = 3.14$

$C = perimeter$

$\longleftrightarrow = circumference$

centre

Check What You Know

Adding and Subtracting Rational Numbers

Evaluate each expression.

a	b	c
1. opposite of 45 -45	opposite of –9 9	opposite of –10 10
2. opposite of 21 -21	opposite of 6 -6	opposite of –31 31
3. opposite of 52 -52	opposite of –89 89	opposite of 18 -18
4. $|7| =$ 7	$|-34| =$ -34	$|58| =$ 58
5. $-|35| =$ -35	$-|-56| =$ 56	$|-39| =$ -39

Identify the property of addition described as *commutative, associative,* or *identity.*

6. The sum of any number and zero is the original number. __identity__

7. When two numbers are added, the sum is the same regardless of the order of addends.

__commutative__

8. When three or more numbers are added, the sum is the same regardless of how the addends

are grouped. __associative__

a	b
9. $7 + (1 + 9) = (7 + 1) + 9$	$3 + 0 = 3$
__associative__	__identity__
10. $9 + 5 = 5 + 9$	$8 + 10 = 10 + 8$
__commutative__	__commutative__
11. $6 + (-6) = 0$	$(6 + 3) + 7 = 6 + (3 + 7)$
__identity__	__associative__
12. $15 + 0 = 15$	$13 + 2 = 2 + 13$
__identity__	__commutative__

NAME _____

Check What You Know

Adding and Subtracting Rational Numbers

Add or subtract. Write fractions in simplest form.

	a	b	c	d
13.	$2\frac{1}{4}$ $+2\frac{2}{3}$ $4\frac{11}{12}$	$3\frac{1}{2}$ $+2\frac{1}{7}$ $5\frac{9}{14}$	$2\frac{1}{8}$ $+4\frac{2}{3}$ $6\frac{19}{24}$	$1\frac{5}{7}$ $+2\frac{4}{5}$ $4\frac{18}{35}$
14.	$6\frac{1}{3}$ $-2\frac{1}{4}$ $4\frac{1}{12}$ a	$\frac{3}{8}$ $-\frac{1}{4}$ $\frac{1}{8}$ b	$5\frac{3}{10}$ $-2\frac{4}{5}$ $2\frac{1}{2}$	$3\frac{4}{7}$ $-1\frac{1}{2}$ $2\frac{1}{14}$ c

15. $-3 + 2 =$ __-1__ $3 + (-2) =$ __1__ $7 + (-4) =$ __3__

16. $-8 + (-3) =$ __-11__ $-7 + 6 =$ __-1__ $-4 + (-9) =$ __-13__

17. $6 - 12 =$ __-6__ $3 - (-4) =$ __7__ $-2 - 4 =$ __-6__

SHOW YOUR WORK

Solve each problem.

18. One box of clips weighs $4\frac{2}{3}$ ounces. Another box weighs $5\frac{3}{8}$ ounces. What is the total weight of the two boxes?

The total weights is __10 1/24__ ounces.

18. $4\frac{16}{24} + 5\frac{9}{24} = 9\frac{25}{24}$

Ans: $10\frac{1}{24}$

19. Luggage on a certain airline is limited to 2 pieces per person. Together, the 2 pieces can weigh no more than $58\frac{1}{2}$ pounds. If a passenger has one piece of luggage that weighs $32\frac{1}{3}$ pounds, what is the most the second piece can weigh?

The second piece can weigh __26 1/6__ pounds.

19. $58\frac{1}{2} = 58\frac{3}{6}$

$32\frac{1}{3} = 32\frac{2}{6}$

$58 - 32 = 26$

$3/6 - 2/6 = 1/6$

Ans: $26\frac{1}{6}$

20. Mavis spends $1\frac{1}{4}$ hours on the bus every weekday (Monday through Friday). How many hours is she on the bus each week?

She is on the bus __6 1/4__ hours each week.

20. $1\frac{1}{4} \times \frac{5}{1}$ Ans: $6\frac{1}{4}$

$\frac{5}{4} \times \frac{5}{1} = \frac{25}{4} = 6\frac{1}{4}$

NAME _____

Lesson 1.1 Understanding Absolute Value

The **absolute value** of a number is a number that is the same distance from zero on a number line as the given number, but on the opposite side of zero.

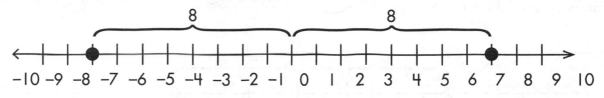

−8 and 8 are absolute value because they are the same distance from zero on opposite sides of the number line.

Evaluate the expressions below.

	a	**b**	**c**
1.	opposite of 19 __−19__	opposite of −7 __7__	opposite of −2 __2__
2.	opposite of 28 __−28__	opposite of −50 __50__	opposite of 10 __−10__
3.	opposite of 92 __−92__	opposite of −31 __31__	opposite of −74 __74__
4.	opposite of 936 __−936__	opposite of 76 __−76__	opposite of 65 __−65__
5.	opposite of −32 __32__	opposite of −36 __36__	opposite of 73 __−73__
6.	opposite of 55 __−55__	opposite of −47 __47__	opposite of 87 __−87__
7.	opposite of −61 __61__	opposite of 37 __−37__	opposite of −23 __23__
8.	opposite of 25 __−25__	opposite of 68 __−68__	opposite of −53 __53__
9.	opposite of 71 __−71__	opposite of −99 __99__	opposite of 90 __−90__
10.	opposite of 40 __−40__	opposite of 44 __−44__	opposite of −77 __77__
11.	opposite of −52 __52__	opposite of 66 __−66__	opposite of −95 __95__
12.	opposite of 15 __−15__	opposite of −20 __20__	opposite of −9 __9__

Lesson 1.2 Absolute Values and Integers

The **absolute value** of a number is the distance between 0 and the number on a number line. Remember that distance is always a positive quantity (or zero). Absolute value is shown by vertical bars on each side of the number.

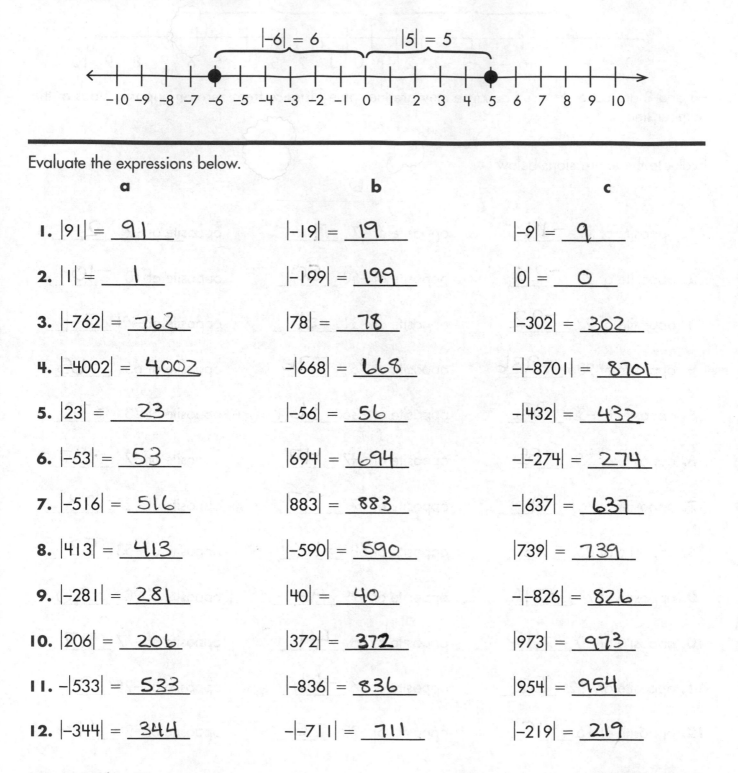

Evaluate the expressions below.

	a	b	c
1.	$\lvert 91 \rvert = \underline{91}$	$\lvert -19 \rvert = \underline{19}$	$\lvert -9 \rvert = \underline{9}$
2.	$\lvert 1 \rvert = \underline{1}$	$\lvert -199 \rvert = \underline{199}$	$\lvert 0 \rvert = \underline{0}$
3.	$\lvert -762 \rvert = \underline{762}$	$\lvert 78 \rvert = \underline{78}$	$\lvert -302 \rvert = \underline{302}$
4.	$\lvert -4002 \rvert = \underline{4002}$	$-\lvert 668 \rvert = \underline{668}$	$-\lvert -8701 \rvert = \underline{8701}$
5.	$\lvert 23 \rvert = \underline{23}$	$\lvert -56 \rvert = \underline{56}$	$-\lvert 432 \rvert = \underline{432}$
6.	$\lvert -53 \rvert = \underline{53}$	$\lvert 694 \rvert = \underline{694}$	$-\lvert -274 \rvert = \underline{274}$
7.	$\lvert -516 \rvert = \underline{516}$	$\lvert 883 \rvert = \underline{883}$	$-\lvert 637 \rvert = \underline{637}$
8.	$\lvert 413 \rvert = \underline{413}$	$\lvert -590 \rvert = \underline{590}$	$\lvert 739 \rvert = \underline{739}$
9.	$\lvert -281 \rvert = \underline{281}$	$\lvert 40 \rvert = \underline{40}$	$-\lvert -826 \rvert = \underline{826}$
10.	$\lvert 206 \rvert = \underline{206}$	$\lvert 372 \rvert = \underline{372}$	$\lvert 973 \rvert = \underline{973}$
11.	$-\lvert 533 \rvert = \underline{533}$	$\lvert -836 \rvert = \underline{836}$	$\lvert 954 \rvert = \underline{954}$
12.	$\lvert -344 \rvert = \underline{344}$	$-\lvert -711 \rvert = \underline{711}$	$\lvert -219 \rvert = \underline{219}$

Lesson 1.3 Subtraction as an Inverse Operation

Subtraction is the same as the process of adding the additive inverse, or opposite, of a number to another number.

$$7 - 4 = 7 + (-4)$$

Write an equivalent equation using the additive inverse.

	a		**b**
1.	$8 - 3 = \underline{8+(-3)}$	$9 - 2 = \underline{9+(-2)}$
2.	$12 + (-7) = \underline{12-7}$	$8 + (-12) = \underline{8-12}$
3.	$52 - 13 = \underline{52+(-13)}$	$23 - 10 = \underline{23+(-10)}$
4.	$67 + (-11) = \underline{67-11}$	$45 + (-6) = \underline{45-6}$
5.	$30 - 15 = \underline{30+(-15)}$	$74 - 23 = \underline{74+(-23)}$
6.	$3 + (-56) = \underline{3-56}$	$62 + (-32) = \underline{62-32}$
7.	$87 - 85 = \underline{87+(-85)}$	$54 - 20 = \underline{54+(-20)}$
8.	$50 + (-17) = \underline{50-17}$	$41 + (-12) = \underline{41-12}$
9.	$89 - 57 = \underline{89+(-57)}$	$46 - 40 = \underline{46+(-40}$
10.	$96 + (-20) = \underline{96-20}$	$94 + (-90) = \underline{94-90}$
11.	$83 - 67 = \underline{83+(-67)}$	$98 - 34 = \underline{98+(-34)}$
12.	$76 + (-20) = \underline{76-20}$	$90 + (-76) = \underline{90-76}$

Lesson 1.4 Adding Fractions and Mixed Numbers

To add fractions or mixed numbers when the denominators are different, rename the fractions so the denominators are the same.

$$\frac{2}{3} = \frac{2}{3} \times \frac{7}{7} = \frac{14}{21}$$
$$+\frac{3}{7} = +\frac{3}{7} \times \frac{3}{3} = +\frac{9}{21}$$
$$\frac{23}{21} = 1\frac{2}{21}$$

$$3\frac{1}{2} = 3\frac{3}{6}$$
$$+2\frac{2}{3} = +2\frac{4}{6}$$
$$5\frac{7}{6} = 6\frac{1}{6}$$

Add. Write each answer in simplest form.

	a	b	c	d
1.	$\frac{3}{4}$ $+\frac{5}{8}$ $1\frac{3}{8}$	$\frac{1}{2}$ $+\frac{1}{3}$ $\frac{5}{6}$	$\frac{3}{4}\frac{15}{20}$ $+\frac{2}{5}\frac{8}{20}$ $\frac{23}{20}$	$\frac{1}{6}$ $+\frac{1}{3}$ $\frac{1}{2}$
2.	$\frac{3}{8}$ $+\frac{4}{5}$ $1\frac{7}{40}$	$\frac{1}{2}$ $+\frac{3}{10}$ $\frac{8}{10}=\frac{4}{5}$	$\frac{2}{3}$ $+\frac{3}{12}$ $\frac{11}{12}$	$\frac{3}{4}$ $+\frac{7}{10}$ $1\frac{9}{20}$
3.	$\frac{1}{4}$ $+\frac{3}{8}$ $\frac{5}{8}$	$\frac{2}{5}$ $+\frac{3}{7}$ $\frac{29}{35}$	$\frac{1}{7}$ $+\frac{7}{8}$ $1\frac{1}{56}$	$\frac{2}{3}$ $+\frac{1}{5}$ $\frac{13}{15}$
4.	$1\frac{1}{3}$ $+2\frac{1}{4}$	$3\frac{3}{8}$ $+7\frac{1}{2}$	$4\frac{2}{7}$ $+2\frac{1}{3}$	$1\frac{2}{5}$ $+3\frac{3}{10}$
5.	$4\frac{4}{9}$ $+3\frac{1}{3}$	$1\frac{1}{8}$ $+1\frac{7}{10}$	$2\frac{1}{6}$ $+3\frac{5}{8}$	$1\frac{3}{7}$ $+2\frac{1}{5}$
6.	$3\frac{1}{2}$ $+2\frac{1}{4}$	$2\frac{5}{6}$ $+1\frac{5}{9}$	$3\frac{4}{7}$ $+1\frac{1}{10}$	$4\frac{1}{3}$ $+2\frac{1}{2}$

Lesson 1.5 Adding Integers

The sum of two positive integers is a positive integer.

$$2 + 5 = 7$$

The sum of two negative integers is a negative integer.

$$-3 + -6 = -9$$

To find the sum of two integers with opposite signs, subtract the digit of lesser value from the digit of greater value and keep the sign of the greater digit.

$$5 + (-3) = 5 - 3 = 2$$

Add.

	a	b	c	d
1.	$3 + 4 \underline{7}$	$-3 + (-4) \underline{-7}$	$3 + (-4) \underline{-1}$	$-3 + 4 \underline{1}$
2.	$-3 + (-3) \underline{-9}$	$3 + (-3) \underline{0}$	$-3 + 3 \underline{0}$	$3 + 3 \underline{6}$
3.	$5 + (-1) \underline{4}$	$-5 + 1 \underline{-4}$	$-5 + (-1) \underline{-6}$	$5 + 1 \underline{6}$
4.	$-7 + 3 \underline{-4}$	$-7 + (-3) \underline{-10}$	$7 + (-3) \underline{4}$	$7 + 3 \underline{10}$
5.	$4 + 7 \underline{11}$	$4 + (-7) \underline{-3}$	$-4 + (7) \underline{3}$	$-4 + (-7) \underline{-11}$
6.	$8 + (-8) \underline{0}$	$-8 + (-8) \underline{-16}$	$8 + 8 \underline{16}$	$-8 + 8 \underline{0}$
7.	$-3 + 0 \underline{-3}$	$3 + 0 \underline{3}$	$-5 + (-6) \underline{-11}$	$-5 + 6 \underline{1}$
8.	$5 + (-6) \underline{-1}$	$5 + 6 \underline{11}$	$-8 + 0 \underline{-8}$	$8 + 0 \underline{8}$
9.	$-3 + 6 \underline{3}$	$-3 + (-6) \underline{-9}$	$3 + 6 \underline{9}$	$3 + (-6) \underline{-3}$
10.	$-6 + (-4) \underline{-10}$	$-6 + 4 \underline{-2}$	$6 + (-4) \underline{2}$	$6 + 4 \underline{10}$

Lesson 1.5 Adding Integers

To find the sum of two integers with different signs, find their absolute values. Remember, **absolute value** is the distance (in units) that a number is from 0, expressed as a positive quantity. Subtract the lesser number from the greater number. Absolute value is written as $|n|$.

The sum has the same sign as the integer with the larger absolute value.

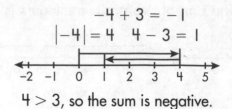

$-4 + 3 = -1$
$|-4| = 4 \quad 4 - 3 = 1$

$4 > 3$, so the sum is negative.

Add.

	a	**b**	**c**
1.	$6 + 2 = \underline{8}$	$9 + (-4) = \underline{5}$	$7 + (-9) = \underline{-2}$
2.	$-4 + 7 = \underline{3}$	$-3 + (-6) = \underline{-9}$	$-12 + 11 = \underline{-1}$
3.	$-16 + 0 = \underline{-16}$	$13 + (-24) = \underline{-11}$	$-6 + 8 = \underline{2}$
4.	$0 + (-9) = \underline{-9}$	$-1 + 2 = \underline{1}$	$1 + (-2) = \underline{-1}$
5.	$-4 + 4 = \underline{0}$	$3 + (-6) = \underline{-3}$	$7 + (-17) = \underline{-10}$
6.	$-45 + 21 = \underline{-24}$	$41 + 44 = \underline{85}$	$33 + 25 = \underline{8}$
7.	$27 + (-39) = \underline{-12}$	$20 + 1 = \underline{21}$	$3 + (-3) = \underline{0}$
8.	$-12 + (-12) = \underline{-24}$	$35 + (-26) = \underline{9}$	$-22 + 16 = \underline{-6}$
9.	$31 + 17 = \underline{48}$	$-9 + (-6) = \underline{-15}$	$-47 + 36 = \underline{-11}$
10.	$4 + 5 = \underline{9}$	$-43 + 35 = \underline{-8}$	$24 + (-33) = \underline{-9}$

Lesson 1.6 Subtracting Integers

To subtract an integer, add its opposite.

$$5 - 7 = 5 + (-7) = -2$$

Subtract.

	a	**b**	**c**
1.	3 – 11 = _____	5 – 2 = _____	–4 – 6 = _____
2.	–12 – 3 = _____	–5 – (–6) = _____	14 – 19 = _____
3.	4 – 19 = _____	–11 – (–1) = _____	16 – (–27) = _____
4.	–6 – (–6) = _____	–11 – 0 = _____	–2 – 2 = _____
5.	8 – 1 = _____	8 – (–1) = _____	–13 – 3 = _____
6.	43 – 15 = _____	–27 – (–39) = _____	–24 – (–38) = _____
7.	–46 – (–31) = _____	–48 – (–47) = _____	–38 – (–17) = _____
8.	9 – (–6) = _____	15 – (–1) = _____	–19 – (–22) = _____
9.	(–3) – 24 = _____	–11 – 44 = _____	42 – 45 = _____
10.	–33 – 12 = _____	–37 – (–40) = _____	5 – (–32) = _____

Lesson 1.6 Subtracting Integers

Subtract.

	a	b	c
1.	−32 − (−27) = _____	−26 − 3 = _____	28 − (−20) = _____
2.	7 − (−37) = _____	−9 − 48 = _____	28 − (−15) = _____
3.	16 − (−1) = _____	24 − (−49) = _____	−30 − (−36) = _____
4.	−44 − 24 = _____	−31 − 34 = _____	−31 − (−13) = _____
5.	−49 − (−46) = _____	−16 − 49 = _____	18 − 28 = _____
6.	−32 − (−50) = _____	−32 − (−21) = _____	−48 − (−47) = _____
7.	−5 − (−30) = _____	14 − (−20) = _____	9 − (−47) = _____
8.	−33 − 39 = _____	4 − (−8) = _____	1 − (−42) = _____
9.	32 − (−41) = _____	40 − 44 = _____	−13 − (−39) = _____
10.	−50 − 19 = _____	48 − (−32) = _____	−14 − (−39) = _____
11.	−18 − (−4) = _____	−45 − 13 = _____	8 − (−67) = _____
12.	56 − (−21) = _____	−11 − 34 = _____	24 − (−17) = _____
13.	31 − (−31) = _____	26 − (−9) = _____	−83 − (−3) = _____
14.	−87 − 6 = _____	−90 − 12 = _____	−46 − (−9) = _____

Lesson 1.7 Subtracting Fractions and Mixed Numbers

To subtract fractions or mixed numbers when the denominators are different, rename the fractions so the denominators are the same.

$$\frac{4}{5} = \frac{4}{5} \times \frac{2}{2} = \frac{8}{10}$$
$$-\frac{1}{10} \qquad -\frac{1}{10} \qquad -\frac{1}{10}$$
$$\frac{7}{10}$$

$$4\frac{1}{4} = 4\frac{1}{4} = 3\frac{5}{4}$$
$$-2\frac{1}{2} \quad -2\frac{2}{4} \quad -2\frac{2}{4}$$
$$1\frac{3}{4}$$

Subtract. Write each answer in simplest form.

	a	b	c	d
1.	$\frac{3}{5}$ $-\frac{1}{4}$	$\frac{1}{2}$ $-\frac{3}{10}$	$\frac{7}{8}$ $-\frac{1}{2}$	$\frac{4}{5}$ $-\frac{1}{3}$
2.	$\frac{5}{6}$ $-\frac{1}{3}$	$\frac{2}{3}$ $-\frac{1}{5}$	$\frac{5}{8}$ $-\frac{1}{6}$	$\frac{7}{10}$ $-\frac{1}{2}$
3.	$\frac{3}{4}$ $-\frac{2}{3}$	$\frac{5}{9}$ $-\frac{1}{2}$	$\frac{1}{2}$ $-\frac{1}{3}$	$\frac{7}{11}$ $-\frac{2}{9}$
4.	$2\frac{3}{8}$ $-1\frac{2}{9}$	$3\frac{1}{4}$ $-1\frac{1}{3}$	$4\frac{1}{2}$ $-3\frac{3}{4}$	$6\frac{5}{8}$ $-4\frac{6}{7}$
5.	$3\frac{2}{11}$ $-1\frac{5}{8}$	$7\frac{2}{3}$ $-3\frac{2}{5}$	$5\frac{1}{3}$ $-2\frac{1}{2}$	$2\frac{5}{6}$ $-1\frac{2}{7}$
6.	$4\frac{7}{9}$ $-2\frac{2}{3}$	$3\frac{1}{5}$ $-1\frac{3}{4}$	$4\frac{5}{6}$ $-2\frac{1}{8}$	$3\frac{1}{8}$ $-1\frac{3}{4}$

Lesson 1.8 Adding Using Mathematical Properties

The **Commutative Property of Addition** states: $a + b = b + a$

The **Associative Property of Addition** states: $(a + b) + c = a + (b + c)$

The **Identity Property of Addition** states: $a + 0 = a$

Rewrite each equation using your knowledge of addition properties.

	a	b

1. $17 + n =$ _____ $n + 0 =$ _____

2. _____ $= (x + y) + 2$ $r + s =$ _____

3. $0 + x =$ _____ $(3 + g) + h =$ _____

4. $(9 + r) + 5 =$ _____ $t + h =$ _____

Solve each equation. Use the properties of addition to help.

5. $11 + 18 + 12 =$ _____ $(5 + 3) + 0 =$ _____

6. $14 + 15 + 16 =$ _____ $(17 + 0) + 2 =$ _____

7. $23 + 24 + 25 =$ _____ $(4 + 5) + 0 =$ _____

8. $54 + 43 + 19 =$ _____ $(8 + 0) + 10 =$ _____

Tell which property is used in each equation (*commutative*, *associative*, or *identity*).

9. $7 + (-7) = 0$ _____ $4 + 6 = 6 + 4$ _____

10. $(11 + 2) + 8 = 11 + (2 + 8)$ _____ $9 + 0 = 9$ _____

11. $6 + (4 + 3) = (6 + 4) + 3$ _____ $5 + 9 = 9 + 5$ _____

12. $15 + 0 = 15$ _____ $18 + 7 = 7 + 18$ _____

Lesson 1.9   Problem Solving

Solve each problem.

1. At closing time, the bakery had $2\frac{1}{4}$ apple pies and $1\frac{1}{2}$ cherry pies left. How much more apple pie than cherry pie was left?

    There was _____ more of an apple pie than cherry.

2. The hardware store sold $6\frac{3}{8}$ boxes of large nails and $7\frac{2}{5}$ boxes of small nails. In total, how many boxes of nails did the store sell?

    The store sold _____ boxes of nails.

3. Nita studied $4\frac{1}{3}$ hours on Saturday and $5\frac{1}{4}$ hours on Sunday. How many hours did she spend studying?

    She spent _____ hours studying.

4. Kwan is $5\frac{2}{3}$ feet tall. Mary is $4\frac{11}{12}$ feet tall. How much taller is Kwan?

    Kwan is _____ foot taller.

5. This week, Jim practiced the piano $1\frac{1}{8}$ hours on Monday and $2\frac{3}{7}$ hours on Tuesday. How many hours did he practice this week? How much longer did Jim practice on Tuesday than on Monday?

    Jim practiced _____ hours this week.

    Jim practiced _____ hours longer on Tuesday.

6. Oscar caught a fish that weighed $4\frac{1}{6}$ pounds and then caught another that weighed $6\frac{5}{8}$ pounds. How much more did the second fish weigh?

    The second fish weighed _____ pounds more.

1.

2.

3.

4.

5.

6.

Lesson 1.9 Problem Solving

SHOW YOUR WORK

Solve each problem.

1. One cake recipe calls for $\frac{2}{3}$ cup of sugar. Another recipe calls for $1\frac{1}{4}$ cups of sugar. How many cups of sugar are needed to make both cakes?

   _____ cups of sugar are needed.

2. Nicole and Daniel are splitting a pizza. Nicole eats $\frac{1}{4}$ of a pizza and Daniel eats $\frac{2}{3}$ of it. How much pizza is left?

   _____ of the pizza is left.

3. The Juarez family is making a cross-country trip. On Saturday, they traveled 450.8 miles. On Sunday, they traveled 604.6 miles. How many miles have they traveled so far?

   They have traveled _____ miles.

4. Kathy's science book is $1\frac{1}{6}$ inches thick. Her reading book is $1\frac{3}{8}$ inches thick. How much thicker is her reading book than her science book?

   It is _____ inches thicker.

5. A large watermelon weighs 10.4 pounds. A smaller watermelon weighs 3.6 pounds. How much less does the smaller watermelon weigh?

   It weighs _____ pounds less.

6. Terrance picked 115.2 pounds of apples on Monday. He picked 97.6 pounds of apples on Tuesday. How many pounds of apples did Terrance pick altogether?

   Terrance picked _____ pounds of apples.

1.
2.
3.
4.
5.
6.

Check What You Learned

Adding and Subtracting Rational Numbers

Evaluate each expression.

	a	b	c

1. opposite of –54 _____   opposite of 19 _____   opposite of 31 _____

2. opposite of –6 _____   opposite of 21 _____   opposite of –10 _____

3. opposite of 54 _____   opposite of –34 _____   opposite of 86 _____

4. $|-35| =$ _____ $-|-43| =$ _____ $|35| =$ _____

5. $-|75| =$ _____ $-|83| =$ _____ $-|99| =$ _____

Identify the property of addition described as *commutative*, *associative*, or *identity*.

6. When two numbers are added, the sum is the same regardless of the order of addends.

_____

7. When three or more numbers are added, the sum is the same regardless of how the addends are grouped.

_____

8. The sum of any number and zero is the original number.

_____

	a	b

9. $4 + 10 = 10 + 4$ _____ $1 + (-1) = 0$ _____

10. $(1 + 8) + 2 = 1 + (8 + 2)$ _____ $3 + 5 = 5 + 3$ _____

11. $8 + 0 = 8$ _____ $2 + (6 + 4) = (2 + 6) + 4$ _____

12. $12 + 9 = 9 + 12$ _____ $(8 + 5) + 3 = 8 + (5 + 3)$ _____

Check What You Learned

Adding and Subtracting Rational Numbers

Add or subtract. Write fractions in simplest form.

	a	b	c	d
13.	$\frac{3}{8}$ $+1\frac{5}{7}$	$2\frac{1}{4}$ $+3\frac{1}{3}$	$1\frac{5}{6}$ $+2\frac{7}{8}$	$4\frac{3}{4}$ $+2\frac{3}{8}$
14.	$4\frac{2}{3}$ $-1\frac{1}{4}$	$\frac{7}{8}$ $-\frac{1}{2}$	$4\frac{3}{10}$ $-1\frac{6}{7}$	$5\frac{1}{4}$ $-2\frac{5}{6}$

	a	b	c
15.	$-6 + 4 =$ _____	$7 + (-3) =$ _____	$-5 + (-2) =$ _____
16.	$-9 + 12 =$ _____	$8 + (-11) =$ _____	$-4 + (-8) =$ _____
17.	$13 - 16 =$ _____	$9 - (-8) =$ _____	$-3 - 7 =$ _____

SHOW YOUR WORK

Solve each problem.

18. A large patio brick weighs $4\frac{3}{8}$ pounds. A small patio brick weighs $2\frac{1}{3}$ pounds. How much more does the large brick weigh?

The large brick weighs _____ pounds more.

18.

19. A small bottle holds $\frac{1}{3}$ of a liter. A large bottle holds $4\frac{1}{2}$ liters. How much more does the large bottle hold?

The large bottle holds _____ liters more.

19.

20. The basketball team practiced $3\frac{1}{4}$ hours on Monday and $2\frac{1}{3}$ hours on Tuesday. How many hours has the team practiced so far this week?

The team has practiced _____ hours this week.

20.

Check What You Know

Multiplying and Dividing Rational Numbers

Rewrite each expression using the distributive property.

                    a   **b**

1. $(x \times 3) + (x \times 7) =$ $8 \times (b + 12) =$

     _X x (3+7)_   _(8 x b)+(8 x 12)_

2. $4 \times (3 + c) =$ $(5 \times m) + (5 \times n) =$

     _(4 x 3)+(4 x c)_   _10 (m+n)_

Identify the property described as *commutative*, *associative*, *identity*, or *zero*.

3. The product of any number and one is that number. ___*identity*___

4. When two numbers are multiplied together, the product is the same regardless of the order

of the factors. ___*Commutative*___

5. When a factor is multiplied by zero, the product is always 0. ___*zero*___

6. When three or more numbers are multiplied together, the product is the same regardless

of how the factors are grouped. ___*associative*___

                    a   **b**

7. $6 \times 0 = 0$ $(5 \times 4) \times 6 = 5 \times (4 \times 6)$

     zero   _associative_

8. $a \times 1 = a$ $8 \times 9 = 9 \times 8$

     identity   _commutative_

Change each rational number into a decimal using long division.

9. $\frac{3}{5} =$ _____ $\frac{4}{8} =$ _____

10. $\frac{1}{4} =$ _____ $\frac{7}{10} =$ _____

Check What You Know

Multiplying and Dividing Rational Numbers

Multiply or divide. Write answers in simplest form.

	a	b	c
11.	$\frac{3}{8} \times \frac{4}{5} =$ _____	$\frac{1}{2} \times \frac{3}{7} =$ _____	$2\frac{3}{4} \times 1\frac{2}{7} =$ _____
12.	$6\frac{1}{8} \div 2\frac{4}{7} =$ _____	$3\frac{2}{3} \div 8 =$ _____	$5\frac{1}{2} \div 1\frac{2}{5} =$ _____
13.	$-3 \times 4 =$ _____	$6 \times (-3) =$ _____	$-2 \times (-8) =$ _____
14.	$-18 \div 9 =$ _____	$24 \div (-6) =$ _____	$-40 \div (-4) =$ _____

SHOW YOUR WORK

Solve each problem.

15. A ribbon that is $22\frac{3}{4}$ inches long must be cut into 7 equal pieces. How long will each piece be?

    Each piece will be _____ inches long.

16. Fifteen cups of flour are to be stored in containers. Each container holds $2\frac{1}{3}$ cups. How many containers will the flour fill? What fraction of another container will it fill?

    The flour will fill _____ full

    containers and _____ of another container.

17. There are $7\frac{1}{2}$ bottles of lemonade. Each bottle holds $1\frac{5}{6}$ quarts. How many quarts of lemonade are there?

    There are _____ quarts of lemonade.

18. If the length of the pool is $14\frac{1}{2}$ feet, the width is $6\frac{1}{2}$ feet, and the depth is $6\frac{1}{2}$ feet, what is the volume of the pool?

    The volume of the pool is _____ cubic feet.

15.

16.

17.

18.

Lesson 2.1 Multiplying and the Distributive Property

The **distributive property** combines multiplication with addition or subtraction. The property states:

$a \times (b + c) = (a \times b) + (a \times c)$ 　　　$3 \times (6 + 4) = (3 \times 6) + (3 \times 4)$

$a \times (b - c) = (a \times b) - (a \times c)$ 　　　　　$3 \times (10) = (18) + (12)$

　　　　　　　　　　　　　　　　　　　　　　$30 = 30$

Rewrite each expression using the distributive property.

a	**b**
1. $(a \times 4) + (a \times 3) =$	$b \times (6 + 12) =$
2. $4 \times (a + b) =$	$(3 \times a) + (3 \times b) =$
3. $(d \times 5) - (d \times 2) =$	$5 \times (8 + p) =$
4. $d \times (8 - h) =$	$12 \times (s - 10) =$
5. $r \times (16 + s) =$	$(35 \times t) + (35 \times y) =$
6. $(8 \times a) + (b \times 8) =$	$r \times (q - s) =$
7. $(6 \times 12) - (w \times 6) =$	$p \times (15 + z) =$
8. $15 \times (y + 0) =$	$(d \times d) + (d \times b) =$
9. $(a \times 2) + (a \times 3) + (a \times 4) =$	$p \times (a + b + 4) =$
10. $(a \times b) + (a \times c) - (a \times d) =$	$8 \times (a + b + c) =$

Lesson 2.2 Multiplying Fractions and Mixed Numbers

Reduce to simplest form if possible. Then, multiply the numerators and multiply the denominators.

$$\frac{3}{8} \times \frac{5}{6} \times \frac{1}{7} = \frac{\overset{1}{\cancel{3}} \times 5 \times 1}{8 \times \underset{2}{\cancel{6}} \times 7} = \frac{1 \times 5 \times 1}{8 \times 2 \times 7} = \frac{5}{112}$$

Rename the numbers as improper fractions. Reduce to simplest form. Multiply the numerators and denominators. Simplify.

$$3\frac{1}{5} \times 2\frac{2}{3} \times 1\frac{1}{8} = \frac{16 \times \overset{1}{\cancel{8}} \times \overset{3}{\cancel{9}}}{5 \times \underset{1}{\cancel{3}} \times \underset{1}{\cancel{8}}} = \frac{16 \times 1 \times 3}{5 \times 1 \times 1} = \frac{48}{5} = 9\frac{3}{5}$$

Multiply. Write each answer in simplest form.

	a	b	c	d
1.	$\frac{1}{2} \times \frac{3}{4}$	$\frac{2}{3} \times \frac{4}{5}$	$\frac{3}{4} \times \frac{3}{4}$	$\frac{4}{5} \times \frac{1}{8}$
2.	$\frac{3}{5} \times \frac{7}{8}$	$\frac{1}{3} \times \frac{3}{5}$	$\frac{3}{7} \times \frac{1}{5}$	$\frac{3}{10} \times \frac{4}{5}$
3.	$\frac{5}{8} \times \frac{3}{8}$	$\frac{2}{3} \times \frac{1}{2}$	$\frac{5}{6} \times \frac{2}{3}$	$\frac{4}{7} \times \frac{1}{3}$
4.	$3 \times 1\frac{2}{7}$	$2\frac{1}{4} \times 3\frac{1}{3}$	$1\frac{1}{9} \times 3\frac{1}{4}$	$2\frac{1}{4} \times 6$
5.	$1\frac{2}{3} \times 3\frac{7}{8}$	$2\frac{1}{7} \times 1\frac{1}{3}$	$4\frac{1}{2} \times 2\frac{1}{3} \times 3$	$5\frac{1}{4} \times 2\frac{1}{2} \times 1\frac{1}{3}$
6.	$4\frac{1}{8} \times 3\frac{2}{7} \times 7$	$\frac{5}{6} \times 1\frac{1}{3} \times 2$	$\frac{2}{3} \times 1\frac{5}{8} \times 3\frac{1}{4}$	$1\frac{1}{2} \times 2\frac{2}{3} \times 1\frac{1}{8}$

Lesson 2.3 Multiplying Integers

The product of two integers with the same
sign is positive.

$3 \times 3 = 9$
$-3 \times -3 = 9$

The product of two integers with different
signs is negative.

$3 \times (-3) = -9$
$-3 \times 3 = -9$

Multiply.

	a	b	c	d

1. $3 \times 2 =$ _____ $-4 \times 6 =$ _____ $8 \times (-3) =$ _____ $-3 \times (-4) =$ _____

2. $-8 \times 7 =$ _____ $6 \times (-5) =$ _____ $-3 \times (-8) =$ _____ $-4 \times 11 =$ _____

3. $16 \times (-2) =$ _____ $-4 \times (-1) =$ _____ $8 \times (-11) =$ _____ $-7 \times (-10) =$ _____

4. $5 \times 8 =$ _____ $6 \times (-6) =$ _____ $-13 \times (-2) =$ _____ $-9 \times 9 =$ _____

5. $17 \times (-1) =$ _____ $5 \times (-2) =$ _____ $-14 \times 3 =$ _____ $-7 \times (-5) =$ _____

6. $(-6) \times 0 =$ _____ $7 \times 3 =$ _____ $6 \times (-10) =$ _____ $(-3) \times (-5) =$ _____

7. $8 \times (-2) =$ _____ $(-4) \times (-10) =$ _____ $10 \times (-3) =$ _____ $3 \times 5 =$ _____

8. $9 \times (-4) =$ _____ $10 \times 4 =$ _____ $10 \times (-4) =$ _____ $5 \times 9 =$ _____

9. $0 \times (-10) =$ _____ $11 \times 11 =$ _____ $2 \times 3 =$ _____ $(-4) \times (-12) =$ _____

10. $(-4) \times (-6) =$ _____ $(-10) \times (-2) =$ _____ $3 \times 12 =$ _____ $4 \times 7 =$ _____

Lesson 2.3 Multiplying Integers

Multiply.

	a	**b**	**c**
1.	$2 \times 4 =$ _____	$3 \times (-3) =$ _____	$-12 \times (-12) =$ _____
2.	$9 \times (-7) =$ _____	$9 \times 8 =$ _____	$4 \times (-12) =$ _____
3.	$10 \times (-1) =$ _____	$7 \times 4 =$ _____	$6 \times (-5) =$ _____
4.	$(-2) \times 1 =$ _____	$(-11) \times 2 =$ _____	$12 \times 3 =$ _____
5.	$11 \times 2 =$ _____	$7 \times 11 =$ _____	$(-12) \times 7 =$ _____
6.	$8 \times 5 =$ _____	$11 \times 7 =$ _____	$1 \times (-6) =$ _____
7.	$6 \times (-2) =$ _____	$9 \times (-4) =$ _____	$(-4) \times (-3) =$ _____
8.	$2 \times 7 =$ _____	$3 \times 8 =$ _____	$3 \times (-7) =$ _____
9.	$(-6) \times (-3) =$ _____	$(-8) \times 8 =$ _____	$2 \times 5 =$ _____
10.	$6 \times 9 =$ _____	$(-4) \times 8 =$ _____	$6 \times (-5) =$ _____
11.	$12 \times 32 =$ _____	$7 \times (-14) =$ _____	$-19 \times (-4) =$ _____
12.	$11 \times (-41) =$ _____	$4 \times 33 =$ _____	$18 \times (-18) =$ _____
13.	$11 \times (-46) =$ _____	$21 \times 4 =$ _____	$13 \times (-5) =$ _____
14.	$(-27) \times 16 =$ _____	$(-11) \times 36 =$ _____	$(-6) \times (-92) =$ _____

Lesson 2.4 Dividing Fractions and Mixed Numbers

To divide by a fraction, multiply by its reciprocal.

$$\frac{2}{3} \div \frac{5}{8} = \frac{2}{3} \times \frac{8}{5} = \frac{16}{15} = 1\frac{1}{15} \qquad\qquad 1\frac{2}{3} \div 2\frac{5}{9} = \frac{5}{\cancel{3}} \times \frac{\cancel{9}^{3}}{23} = \frac{15}{23}$$

Divide. Write each answer in simplest form.

	a	b	c	d
1.	$3\frac{1}{2} \div \frac{2}{3} = 5\frac{1}{4}$	$4\frac{3}{4} \div 1\frac{7}{8} = 2\frac{8}{15}$	$\frac{3}{4} \div \frac{1}{2} = 1\frac{1}{2}$	$2\frac{2}{3} \div \frac{1}{8} = 21\frac{1}{3}$
	$\frac{7}{2} \times \frac{3}{2} = \frac{21}{4}$	$\frac{19}{4} \times \frac{8^2}{15} = \frac{38}{15}$	$\frac{3}{4}_2 \times \frac{2^1}{1} = \frac{3}{2}$	$\frac{8}{3} \times \frac{8}{1} = \frac{64}{3}$
2.	$7 \div \frac{3}{5} = 11\frac{2}{3}$	$2\frac{1}{12} \div 1\frac{1}{3} = 1\frac{9}{16}$	$2\frac{1}{7} \div \frac{3}{4} = 2\frac{6}{7}$	$3 \div 5 = 1\frac{2}{5}$
	$\frac{7}{1} \times \frac{5}{3} = \frac{35}{3}$	$\frac{25}{\cancel{12}_4} \times \frac{\cancel{31}}{4} = \frac{25}{16}$	$\frac{\cancel{15}^5}{7} \times \frac{4}{\cancel{3}_1} = \frac{20}{7}$	$\frac{3}{1} \times \frac{1}{5} = \frac{3}{5}$
3.	$1\frac{1}{8} \div \frac{1}{10} = 11\frac{2}{8}$	$1\frac{2}{5} \div 2\frac{1}{3} = 3/5$	$5 \div 1\frac{1}{2} = $ ____	$3\frac{1}{4} \div 1\frac{1}{2} = $ ____
	$\frac{9}{8} \times \frac{10}{1} = \frac{90}{8}$	$\frac{\cancel{7}}{5} \times \frac{3}{\cancel{7}} = \frac{3}{5}$		
4.	$6\frac{2}{3} \div \frac{2}{3} = $ ____	$3\frac{1}{8} \div \frac{2}{7} = $ ____	$4\frac{1}{4} \div \frac{1}{12} = $ ____	$14 \div \frac{1}{7} = $ ____
5.	$2\frac{3}{5} \div 1\frac{2}{7} = $ ____	$1\frac{1}{9} \div \frac{7}{11} = $ ____	$12 \div 15 = $ ____	$2\frac{4}{5} \div 3 = $ ____

Lesson 2.5 Understanding Integer Division

Because multiplication and division are inverse operations, you can use what you know about integer multiplication to solve division problems.

$$-6 \div 2 = x$$
$$-6 = x \times 2$$
$$x = -3$$

Use multiplication as an inverse operation to solve the following integer division problems.

a	b

1. $18 \div (-2) =$ _____ $-7 \div 1 =$ _____

Inverse operation: _____   Inverse operation: _____

2. $20 \div (-4) =$ _____ $-84 \div (-6) =$ _____

Inverse operation: _____   Inverse operation: _____

3. $15 \div (-3) =$ _____ $-54 \div (-9) =$ _____

Inverse operation: _____   Inverse operation: _____

4. $-25 \div 5 =$ _____ $-39 \div (-13) =$ _____

Inverse operation: _____   Inverse operation: _____

5. $81 \div (-9) =$ _____ $-48 \div 4 =$ _____

Inverse operation: _____   Inverse operation: _____

6. $-72 \div 8 =$ _____ $36 \div (-12) =$ _____

Inverse operation: _____   Inverse operation: _____

7. $22 \div (-11) =$ _____ $18 \div (-6) =$ _____

Inverse operation: _____   Inverse operation: _____

Lesson 2.6 Dividing Integers

The quotient of two integers with the same sign is positive.

$8 \div 2 = 4$
$-8 \div (-2) = 4$

The quotient of two integers with different signs is negative.

$8 \div (-2) = -4$
$-8 \div 2 = -4$

Divide.

	a	b	c
1.	$12 \div 4 = $ ____	$16 \div (-4) = $ ____	$-8 \div 4 = $ ____
2.	$7 \div (-1) = $ ____	$-14 \div 7 = $ ____	$24 \div (-6) = $ ____
3.	$81 \div (-3) = $ ____	$-63 \div 9 = $ ____	$-55 \div (-5) = $ ____
4.	$21 \div (-7) = $ ____	$-38 \div 2 = $ ____	$-19 \div (-1) = $ ____
5.	$12 \div (-12) = $ ____	$42 \div (-21) = $ ____	$-60 \div (-10) = $ ____
6.	$20 \div 2 = $ ____	$30 \div (-10) = $ ____	$(-50) \div (-10) = $ ____
7.	$288 \div (-18) = $ ____	$(-85) \div (-5) = $ ____	$(-36) \div 4 = $ ____
8.	$136 \div (-8) = $ ____	$(-171) \div 19 = $ ____	$240 \div 15 = $ ____
9.	$168 \div 12 = $ ____	$(-200) \div 20 = $ ____	$14 \div (-7) = $ ____
10.	$240 \div (-15) = $ ____	$(-120) \div (-8) = $ ____	$102 \div (-17) = $ ____

Lesson 2.6 Dividing Integers

Divide.

	a	**b**	**c**
1.	$(-140) \div (-10) = $ ____	$(-210) \div 15 = $ ____	$(-224) \div (-14) = $ ____
2.	$(-13) \div (-1) = $ ____	$120 \div 8 = $ ____	$144 \div (-8) = $ ____
3.	$400 \div (-20) = $ ____	$39 \div (-13) = $ ____	$(-3) \div 1 = $ ____
4.	$(-200) \div 10 = $ ____	$224 \div (-16) = $ ____	$66 \div 11 = $ ____
5.	$88 \div 11 = $ ____	$(-60) \div 12 = $ ____	$288 \div 16 = $ ____
6.	$288 \div (-16) = $ ____	$(-90) \div 6 = $ ____	$90 \div (-10) = $ ____
7.	$133 \div 19 = $ ____	$55 \div 5 = $ ____	$128 \div 8 = $ ____
8.	$48 \div (-8) = $ ____	$(-306) \div 17 = $ ____	$(-64) \div 4 = $ ____
9.	$35 \div 5 = $ ____	$34 \div (-17) = $ ____	$252 \div (-14) = $ ____
10.	$51 \div 3 = $ ____	$(-18) \div (-9) = $ ____	$(-33) \div (-3) = $ ____
11.	$176 \div 11 = $ ____	$(-180) \div 15 = $ ____	$(-105) \div (-7) = $ ____
12.	$(-96) \div 12 = $ ____	$26 \div (-2) = $ ____	$(-54) \div (-9) = $ ____
13.	$(-156) \div (-12) = $ ____	$(-248) \div 4 = $ ____	$(-272) \div (-34) = $ ____
14.	$(-1037) \div (-17) = $ ____	$688 \div 8 = $ ____	$1008 \div (-42) = $ ____

Lesson 2.7 Multiplying and Dividing Using Mathematical Properties

Commutative Property: The order in which numbers are multiplied does not change the product. $a \times b = b \times a$

Associative Property: The grouping of factors does not change the product. $a \times (b \times c) = (a \times b) \times c$

Identity Property: The product of a factor and 1 is the factor. $a \times 1 = a$

Properties of Zero: The product of a factor and 0 is 0. The quotient of the dividend 0 and any divisor is 0. $a \times 0 = 0 \quad 0 \div a = 0$

Write the name of the property shown by each equation.

a	b

1. $3 \times (2 \times r) = (3 \times 2) \times r$ $15 \times 1 = 15$

_____   _____

2. $12 \times p = p \times 12$ $35 \times 0 = 0$

_____   _____

3. $0 \div 76 = 0$ $(8 \times 9) \times 12 = 8 \times (9 \times 12)$

_____   _____

Rewrite each expression using the property indicated.

4. commutative: $15 \times z$ zero: 16×0

_____   _____

5. identity: $12a \times 1$ associative: $14 \times (3 \times p)$

_____   _____

6. zero: $0 \div 68$ associative: $(6 \times 4) \times n$

_____   _____

NAME _____

Lesson 2.8 Converting Rational Numbers Using Division

Rational numbers can be converted into decimals using long division. All fractions will be turned into decimals that either terminate or repeat.

Terminating

$\frac{1}{8}$ $8\overline{)1.0000}$ 0.1250

Repeating

$\frac{1}{3}$ $3\overline{)1.0000}$ 0.3333

Use long division to change each rational number into a decimal. Then, circle to indicate if each is terminating (T) or repeating (R).

      a   **b**   **c**

1. $\frac{1}{4}$ = _____ T or R $2\frac{3}{5}$ = _____ T or R $\frac{5}{8}$ = _____ T or R

2. $\frac{3}{5}$ = _____ T or R $\frac{7}{200}$ = _____ T or R $\frac{8}{33}$ = _____ T or R

3. $\frac{6}{11}$ = _____ T or R $\frac{7}{50}$ = _____ T or R $4\frac{17}{125}$ = _____ T or R

4. $\frac{7}{20}$ = _____ T or R $\frac{1}{111}$ = _____ T or R $\frac{1}{125}$ = _____ T or R

Lesson 2.8 Converting Rational Numbers Using Division

Rational numbers can be converted into decimals using long division. All fractions will be turned into decimals that either terminate or repeat.

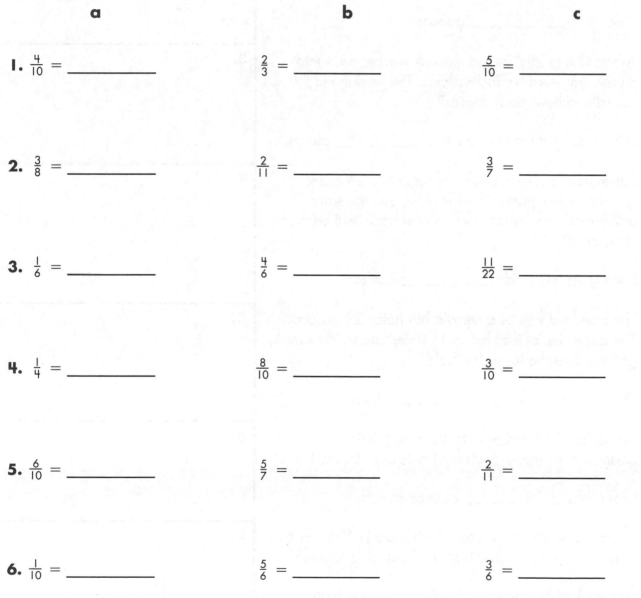

Repeating

$\frac{1}{12}$ $\quad \dfrac{0.08\overline{33}}{12 \overline{)1.0000}}$ Add a line above digits to show they repeat.

Terminating

$\frac{1}{25}$ $\quad \dfrac{0.04}{25 \overline{)1.00}}$

Change each rational number into a decimal using long division. Place a line above any digits which repeat.

	a	b	c
1.	$\frac{4}{10}$ = _____	$\frac{2}{3}$ = _____	$\frac{5}{10}$ = _____
2.	$\frac{3}{8}$ = _____	$\frac{2}{11}$ = _____	$\frac{3}{7}$ = _____
3.	$\frac{1}{6}$ = _____	$\frac{4}{6}$ = _____	$\frac{11}{22}$ = _____
4.	$\frac{1}{4}$ = _____	$\frac{8}{10}$ = _____	$\frac{3}{10}$ = _____
5.	$\frac{6}{10}$ = _____	$\frac{5}{7}$ = _____	$\frac{2}{11}$ = _____
6.	$\frac{1}{10}$ = _____	$\frac{5}{6}$ = _____	$\frac{3}{6}$ = _____

Lesson 2.9 Problem Solving

Solve each problem. Write each answer in simplest form.

1. David worked $7\frac{1}{3}$ hours today and planted 11 trees. It takes him about the same amount of time to plant each tree. How long did it take him to plant each tree?

   It took him _____ hour to plant each tree.

2. A car uses $3\frac{1}{8}$ gallons of gasoline per hour when driving on the highway. How many gallons will it use after $4\frac{2}{3}$ hours?

   It will use _____ gallons.

3. A board was $24\frac{3}{8}$ inches long. A worker cut it into pieces that were $4\frac{7}{8}$ inches long. The worker cut the board into how many pieces?

   The worker cut the board into _____ pieces.

4. Susan must pour $6\frac{1}{2}$ bottles of juice into 26 drink glasses for her party. If each glass gets the same amount of juice, what fraction of a bottle will each glass hold?

   Each glass will hold _____ bottles.

5. The standard size of a certain bin holds $2\frac{2}{3}$ gallons. The large size of that bin is $1\frac{1}{4}$ times larger. How many gallons does the large bin hold?

   The large bin holds _____ gallons.

6. Diana has $3\frac{1}{4}$ bags of nuts. Each bag holds $4\frac{1}{2}$ pounds. How many pounds of nuts does Diana have?

   Diana has _____ pounds of nuts.

7. There is a stack of 7 crates. Each crate is $10\frac{2}{3}$ inches high. How many inches high is the stack of crates?

   The stack of crates is _____ inches high.

1.

2.

3.

4.

5.

6.

7.

Lesson 2.9 Problem Solving

SHOW YOUR WORK

Solve each problem. Write each answer in simplest form.

1. Each month, Kelsey donates $\frac{1}{5}$ of her allowance to her school for supplies. $\frac{1}{2}$ of that amount goes to the chorus class. How much of her allowance goes to supplies for the chorus class?

   _____ of her allowance goes to help the chorus classes.

2. Alvin cuts $\frac{3}{4}$ of a piece of cheese. He gives $\frac{1}{8}$ of it to Matt. How much of the cheese does Alvin give to Matt?

   Alvin gives _____ of the cheese to Matt.

3. Katie has $16\frac{3}{4}$ hours to finish 3 school projects. How much time may she spend on each project, if she plans to spend the same amount of time on each?

   Katie will spend _____ hours on each project.

4. Martha spent $2.90 on $3\frac{1}{2}$ pounds of bananas. How much did she spend on each pound of bananas?

   She spent _____ on each pound.

5. Monica has $5\frac{1}{2}$ cups of sugar to make pies. If each pie uses $\frac{1}{3}$ cup of sugar, how many pies can Monica make?

   Monica can make _____ pies.

6. Vince has $12\frac{1}{2}$ hours to mow the lawn, do the laundry, make dinner, and finish his homework. How much time can Vince spend on each task, if he plans to spend the same amount of time on each?

   Vince will spend _____ hours on each project.

7. Drew spent $38.97 on $3\frac{1}{4}$ pounds of shrimp. How much did he spend on each pound of shrimp?

   Drew spent _____ on each pound of shrimp.

1.	
2.	
3.	
4.	
5.	
6.	
7.	

Check What You Learned

Multiplying and Dividing Rational Numbers

Rewrite each expression using the distributive property.

a	b
1. $7 \times (10 + a) =$	$(2 \times c) + (2 \times d) =$
_____	_____
2. $(y \times 2) + (y \times 6) =$	$5 \times (k + 4) =$
_____	_____

Identify the property described as *commutative*, *associative*, *identity*, or *zero*.

3. When three or more numbers are multiplied together, the product is the same regardless of how the factors are grouped. _____

4. When zero is divided by any number, the quotient is always 0. _____

5. The product of any number and 1 is that number. _____

6. When two numbers are multiplied together, the product is the same regardless of the order of the factors. _____

a	b
7. $y \times x = x \times y$	$(a \times b) \times c = a \times (b \times c)$
_____	_____
8. $5 \times 1 = 5$	$0 \div 6 = 0$
_____	_____

Change each rational number into a decimal using long division. Place a line over digits which repeat.

a	b
9. $\frac{2}{9} =$ _____	$\frac{4}{9} =$ _____
10. $\frac{1}{11} =$ _____	$\frac{2}{5} =$ _____

Check What You Learned

Multiplying and Dividing Rational Numbers

Multiply or divide. Write answers in simplest form.

	a	**b**	**c**
11.	$\frac{3}{4} \times \frac{1}{6} =$ _____	$\frac{5}{7} \times \frac{2}{3} =$ _____	$5\frac{1}{2} \times 1\frac{1}{4} =$ _____
12.	$5\frac{1}{4} \div 1\frac{3}{8} =$ _____	$6\frac{4}{7} \div 12 =$ _____	$1\frac{1}{2} \div \frac{3}{5} =$ _____
13.	$7 \times (-6) =$ _____	$3 \times (-4) =$ _____	$-5 \times (-2) =$ _____
14.	$12 \div (-4) =$ _____	$-15 \div (-5) =$ _____	$-21 \div 7 =$ _____

SHOW YOUR WORK

Solve each problem.

15. A bucket that holds $5\frac{1}{4}$ gallons of water is being used to fill a tub that can hold $34\frac{1}{8}$ gallons. How many buckets will be needed to fill the tub?

_____ buckets are needed to fill the tub.

15.

16. A black piece of pipe is $8\frac{1}{3}$ centimeters long. A silver piece of pipe is $2\frac{3}{5}$ times longer. How long is the silver piece of pipe?

The silver piece is _____ centimeters long.

16.

17. One section of wood is $3\frac{5}{8}$ meters long. Another section is twice that long. When the two pieces are put together, how long is the piece of wood that is created?

The piece of wood is _____ meters long.

17.

18. Danielle wants to fill a box with dirt to start a garden. If the box is $2\frac{1}{5}$ feet long, by $1\frac{1}{3}$ feet wide, and $1\frac{1}{2}$ feet deep, how much dirt does Danielle need to fill up the box for her garden?

Danielle needs _____ cubic feet of dirt.

18.

NAME _____

Check What You Know

Expressions, Equations, and Inequalities

Rewrite each expression using the property indicated.

a	**b**
1. associative: $(5 + 6) + 7$	identity: 56×1
$5 + (6 + 7)$	
2. zero: $0 \div 4$	commutative: 8×9
	9×8
3. distributive: $3 \times (5 - 2)$	associative: $(7 \times 2) \times 3$
$(3 \times 5) - (3 \times 2)$	$7 \times (2 \times 3)$

Write each phrase as an expression or equation.

4. five less than a number

eight more than a number

5. a number divided by six

the product of two and a number

6. the sum of 3 and a number is 12

six less than a number is nineteen

7. thirty divided by a number is three

the product of 5 and a number is fifteen

8. the product of 5 and a number

the sum of 6 and a number is 16

9. 19 less than a number

27 divided by a number is 9

10. 12 less than a number is 5

the product of 6 and a number is 72

Check What You Know

Expressions, Equations, and Inequalities

Solve each problem.

11. Alicia had $22 to spend on pencils. If each pencil costs $1.50, how many pencils can she buy?

Let p represent the cost of each pencil.

Equation or Inequality: _____

Alicia can buy _____ pencils.

11.

12. The sum of three consecutive even numbers is 51. What is the smallest of these numbers?

Let n represent the smallest number of the set.

Equation or Inequality: _____

The smallest of these numbers is _____.

12.

13. Mark bought 8 boxes. A week later, half of all his boxes were destroyed in a fire. There are now only 20 boxes left. With how many did he start?

Let b represent how many boxes he started with.

Equation or inequality: _____

Mark began with _____ boxes.

13.

14. Jillian sold half of her comic books and then bought 15 more. She now has 30. With how many did she begin?

Let c represent the number of comic books with which she began.

Equation or inequality: _____

Jillian began with _____ CDs.

14.

15. On Tuesday, Shanice bought 5 new pens. On Wednesday, half of all the pens that she had were accidentally thrown away. On Thursday, there were only 16 left. How many did she have on Monday?

Let p represent the number of pens she had on Monday.

Equation or inequality: _____

Shanice had _____ pens on Monday.

15.

Lesson 3.1 Mathematical Properties & Equivalent Expressions

Commutative Property: The order in which numbers are added does not change the sum. The order in which numbers are multiplied does not change the product.

$a + b = b + a$
$a \times b = b \times a$

Associative Property: The grouping of addends does not change the sum. The grouping of factors does not change the product.

$a + (b + c) = (a + b) + c$
$a \times (b \times c) = (a \times b) \times c$

Identity Property: The sum of an addend and 0 is the addend. The product of a factor and 1 is the factor.

$a + 0 = a$
$a \times 1 = a$

Properties of Zero: The product of a factor and 0 is 0. The quotient of the dividend 0 and any divisor is 0.

$a \times 0 = 0$
$0 \div a = 0$

Distributive Property: If two addends or the minuend and subtrahend in an equation are being multiplied by the same factor, the equation can be rewritten by factoring out the common factor.

$a \times (b + c) = (a \times b) + (a \times c)$
$a \times (b - c) = (a \times b) - (a \times c)$

Rewrite each expression using the property indicated.

a

1. associative: $(7 + 6) + y =$

$7 + (6 + y)$

2. commutative: $z \times 8 =$

8×2

3. distributive: $6 \times (a + b) =$

$(6 \times a) + (6 \times b)$

4. commutative: $7 + y =$

$y + 7$

5. identity: $45 \times 1 =$

45

b

identity: $724 + 0 =$

724

zero: $61 \times 0 =$

0

zero: $0 \div 5 =$

0

associative: $5 \times (6 \times 3) =$

$(5 \times 6) \times 3$

distributive: $(7 \times 3) + (7 \times 7) =$

$7(3 + 7)$

Lesson 3.1 Mathematical Properties & Equivalent Expressions

Use phrases to help you understand which operations to use in word problems.

Addition Phrases	Subtraction Phrases	Multiplication Phrases	Division Phrases
more than	less than	the product of	the quotient of
the sum of	decreased by	times	divided by

Write each phrase as an expression or equation.

a	b

1. three increased by d

$d+3$

the product of eight and w

$8 \times w$

2. seven less than 12

$12-7$

two more than a number is nine

$n+2=9$

3. a number divided by 6 is 8

$n \div 6 = 8$

nine more than 15

$15+9$

4. the sum of five and six is eleven

$5+6=11$

the quotient of twelve and s is 4

$12 \div s = 4$

5. three less than t is five

$t-3=5$

the product of two and b is 4

$2 \times b = 4$

6. the product of five and three is y

$5 \times 3 = y$

twenty divided by a number is five

$20 \div w = 5$

7. 12 more than 20

$12+20$

the sum of 4 and 11 is 15

$4+11=15$

8. the quotient of 30 and f is 3

$30 \div f = 3$

7 times b is 63

$7 \times b = 63$

Lesson 3.2 Solving Problems with Equivalent Expressions

Sometimes, it is easier to solve equations by writing them in different ways.

A number increased by 10% can be
written as:

- $n + (0.10 \times n)$
- $1.10 \times n$

A number divided by 7 equals 3 can be
written as:

- $n \div 7 = 3$
- $3 \times 7 = n$

Write two equivalent expressions for each statement.

a	b

1. a number decreased by 7%

_____

_____

9 times the sum of 7 and a number

_____

_____

2. $25 plus a 5% tip

_____

_____

the sum of a number and 4 times the number

_____

_____

3. a number divided by 5 equals 9

_____

_____

a number increased by $\frac{1}{5}$

_____

_____

4. 12 times the difference of 15 and a number

_____

_____

$44 plus a 20% tip

_____

_____

5. the sum of 7 and a number times 10

_____

_____

a number decreased by $3\frac{1}{4}$

_____

_____

Lesson 3.3 Creating Expressions to Solve Problems

Write expressions to solve problems by putting the unknown number, or **variable**, on one side of the equation and the known values on the other side of the equation. Then, solve for the value of the variable.

Francine is making earrings and necklaces for six friends. Each pair of earrings uses 6 centimeters of wire and each necklace uses 30 centimeters. How much wire will Francine use?

Let w represent the amount of wire used.
Equation: $w = 6 \times (6 + 30)$
Another way of writing this expression is: $w = (6 \times 6) + (6 \times 30)$
How much wire did Francine use? $w = 216$ centimeters

SHOW YOUR WORK

Solve each problem.

1. A jaguar can run 40 miles per hour while a giraffe can run 32 miles per hour. If they both run for 4 hours, how much farther will the jaguar run?

   Let d represent the distance.

   Equation: _____

   Another way of writing this is: _____

   The jaguar will run _____ miles farther.

   1.

2. Charlene sold 15 magazine subscriptions for the school fundraiser. Mark sold 17 subscriptions and Paul sold 12. How many magazine subscriptions did they sell in all?

   Let s represent subscriptions.

   Equation: _____

   Another way of writing this is: _____

   They sold _____ subscriptions in all.

   2.

3. Shara bought 3 bags of chocolate candies for $1.25 each and 3 bags of gummy bears for $2.00 each. How much did she spend in all?

   Let m represent the money spent.

   Equation: _____

   Another way of writing this is: _____

   Shara spent _____ on candy.

   3.

Lesson 3.3 Problem Solving

Solve each problem.

1. Elsa sold 37 pairs of earrings for $20 each at the craft fair. She is going to use $\frac{1}{4}$ of the money to buy new CDs and is going to put the rest of the money in her savings account. How much money will she put into her savings account?

   Let s stand for the amount of money saved.

   Equation: _____

   How much money did she spend on CDs? _____

   How much money did she put in her savings account?

   _____

   1.

2. Jason deposits $5 into his savings account twice a week for 6 weeks. How much money will he have saved after 6 weeks?

   Let s stand for the amount of money saved.

   Equation: _____

   How much money did he save? _____

   2.

3. Four friends went to the movies. Each ticket cost $8 and each person bought popcorn and a soda for $5. How much did they spend in all?

   Let m stand for the amount of money spent.

   Equation: _____

   What is another way to write the above equation?

   _____

   How much money did they spend? _____

   3.

4. An online store increased the price of a shirt by 17% and charged $3 to ship the shirt to a customer. The customer paid $43 for the shirt. What was the original price of the shirt?

   Let p stand for the price of the shirt.

   Equation: _____

   How much was the shirt before the increase and shipping?

   _____

   4.

5. David and Eric went out to dinner. Their total bill was $45. They added 20% gratuity to the bill. If they split the bill in half, how much did each person spend?

   Let t stand for the amount each person spent.

   Equation: _____

   How much money did each person spend? _____

   5.

Lesson 3.4 Using Variables to Solve Problems

Write an equation to represent the problem, using the variable *n* for the unknown number. Then, solve for the value of the variable. Look at the following problem as an example.

George and Cindy are saving for bicycles. Cindy has saved $15 less than twice as much as George has saved. Together, they have saved $120. How much did each of them save?

Let *n* stand for the amount George has saved. What stands for the amount Cindy has saved? __2n − 15__ What equals the total amount? __n + (2n − 15) = 120__

Simplify: ___3n − 15 = 120___ Solve.

How much has George saved? __$45__
How much has Cindy saved? __$75__

SHOW YOUR WORK

Solve each problem.

1. Nate and Laura picked apples. Laura picked $\frac{1}{2}$ as many as Nate picked. Together they picked 90 apples. How many did each of them pick?

   Let *n* stand for the number Nate picked.
   Equation: __1.5 × n = 90__
   How many apples did Nate pick? __60__
   How many apples did Laura pick? __30__

   1. $n \div 2$
   $n + (n \div 2) = 90$
   $2n \div 2 = 90$
   $n = 90$
   $n = 60$

2. Jordan travels ___half___ of a mile longer to school each day than Harrison does. Combined, they travel $5\frac{1}{4}$ miles to school. How far does each travel?

   Let *n* stand for the distance Jordan travels.
   Equation: _____
   How far does Jordan travel? _____
   How far does Harrison travel? _____

   2.

3. Two jackets have a combined cost of $98. Jacket A costs $12 less than Jacket B. How much does each jacket cost?

   Let *n* stand for the cost of Jacket A.
   Equation: _____
   Jacket A costs _____.
   Jacket B costs _____.

   3.

Lesson 3.4 Problem Solving

SHOW YOUR WORK

Solve each problem.

1. William purchased a new car. The total price he will pay for the car, including interest, is $17,880. If he splits his car payments over 60 months, how much will he pay each month?

   Let p represent each payment.

   Equation: _____

   William will pay _____ each month.

2. Tracy has $1.55 in quarters and dimes. If she has 3 quarters, how many dimes does she have?

   Let d represent the number of dimes.

   Equation: _____

   Tracy has _____ dimes.

3. Kavon is saving money to buy a bicycle that costs $150. He has been saving his $5 weekly allowance for the last 8 weeks and he saved $50 from his birthday money. How much more money does Kavon need to buy his bicycle?

   Let m represent the money Kavon needs.

   Equation: _____

   Kavon needs _____.

4. Lincoln Middle School won their football game last week by scoring 23 points. If they scored two 7-point touchdowns, how many 3-point field goals did they score?

   Let f represent the number of field goals.

   Equation: _____

   They scored _____ field goals.

5. Walker is reading a book that is 792 pages. He reads 15 pages a day during the week, and 25 pages a day during the weekend. After 5 weeks of reading, how many pages does Walker still have left to read before he finishes the book?

   Let r represent the pages left to read.

   Equation: _____

   Walker has _____ pages left to read.

1.

2.

3.

4.

5.

Lesson 3.4 Problem Solving

Solve each problem.

1. Peaches are on sale at the farmer's market for $1.75 per pound. If Ida buys $8.75 worth of peaches, how many pounds of peaches did she buy?

Let p represent pounds of peaches.

Equation: _____

Ida bought _____ pounds of peaches.

2. Kylie makes $8.50 an hour working at a restaurant. If she brings home $170 in her paycheck, how many hours did she work?

Let h represent the number of hours Kylie works.

Equation: _____

Kylie worked _____ hours.

3. Larry and 3 friends went to a basketball game. They paid $5.00 for each of their tickets and each bought a bag of candy. If they spent a total of $28, how much was each bag of candy?

Let c represent bags of candy.

Equation: _____

Each bag of candy cost _____.

4. Three hoses are connected end to end. The first hose is 6.25 feet. The second hose is 6.5 feet. If the length of all 3 hoses when connected is 20 feet, how long is the third hose?

Let h represent the length of the third hose.

Equation: _____

The third hose is _____ feet long.

5. Quinn and her mom went to the movies. They paid $10.50 for each of their tickets and each bought a tub of popcorn. If they spent a total of $38.50, how much was each tub of popcorn?

Let p represent tubs of popcorn.

Equation: _____

Each tub of popcorn cost _____.

1.

2.

3.

4.

5.

Lesson 3.5 Using Variables to Express Inequalities

An **inequality** is a mathematical sentence that states that two expressions are not equal.
$2 \times 5 > 6$

Inequalities can be solved the same way as you solve equations.

$-4 \times x \geq -4$
$-4 \times x \div (-4) \geq -4 \div (-4)$
$x \leq 1$

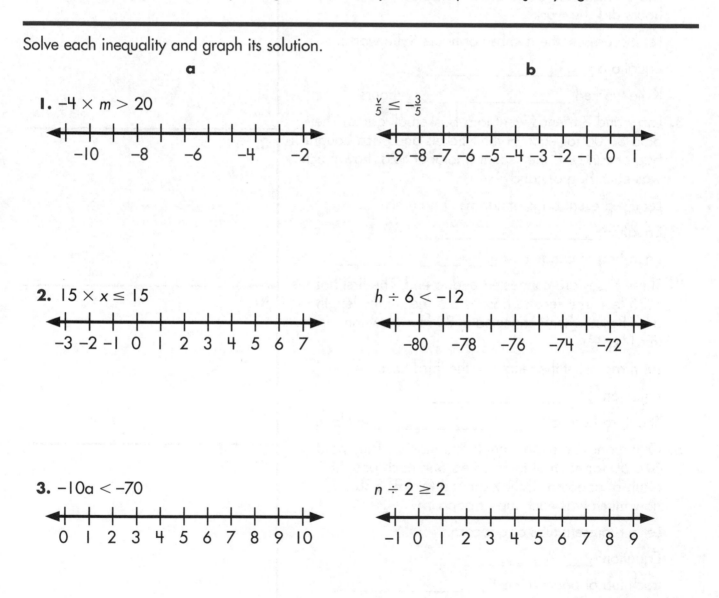

When you multiply or divide by a negative number, you must flip the inequality sign.

Solve each inequality and graph its solution.

a   b

1. $-4 \times m > 20$ $\frac{v}{5} \leq -\frac{3}{5}$

2. $15 \times x \leq 15$ $h \div 6 < -12$

3. $-10a < -70$ $n \div 2 \geq 2$

Lesson 3.5 Using Variables to Express Inequalities

Word problems can be solved by creating inequality statements.

Aria has $55 to spend on flowers. She wants to buy two rose bushes, which will cost $20, and spend the rest of her money on lilies. Each lily costs $10. Write an inequality to show how many lilies Aria can buy.

Let l represent the number of lilies she can buy.
Inequality: $\$10 \times l + \$20 \leq \$55$
$\$10 \times l + \$20 - \$20 \leq \$55 - \$20$
$\$10 \times l \div \$10 \leq \$35 \div \$10$
$l \leq 3.5$
Aria can buy 3 lilies.

SHOW YOUR WORK

Solve each problem by creating an inequality.

1. Andrew had $20 to spend at the fair. If he paid $5 to get into the fair, and rides cost $2 each, what is the maximum number of rides he could go on?

Let r represent the number of rides.

Inequality: _____

Andrew could go on _____ rides.

1.

2. Sandra has $75 to spend on a new outfit. She finds a sweater that costs twice as much the skirt. What is the most the skirt can cost?

Let s represent the cost of the skirt.

Inequality: _____

The most the skirt can cost is _____.

2.

3. Alan earns $7.50 per hour at his after-school jobs. He is saving money to buy a skateboard that costs $120. How many hours will he have to work to earn enough money for the skateboard?

Let h represent the number of hours Alan will have to work.

Inequality: _____

Alan will have to work _____ hours.

3.

Lesson 3.5 Problem Solving

SHOW YOUR WORK

Solve each problem by creating an inequality.

1. Blue Bird Taxi charges a $2.00 flat rate in addition to $0.55 per mile. Marcy only has $10 to spend on a taxi ride. What is the farthest she can ride without going over her limit?

Let *d* equal the distance Marcy can travel.

Inequality: _____

Marcy can travel _____ miles without going over her limit.

1.

2. The school store is selling notebooks for $1.50 and T-shirts for $10.00 to raise money for the school. They have a goal of raising $250 to buy supplies for the science lab. If they have sold 60 notebooks, how many T-shirts will they need to sell to reach their goal?

Let *t* equal the number of T-shirts.

Inequality: _____

They need to sell _____ T-shirts.

2.

3. There are 178 7th grade students and 20 chaperones going on the field trip to the aquarium. Each bus holds 42 people. How many buses will the group have to take?

Let *b* represent the number of buses.

Inequality: _____

They will need to take _____ buses.

3.

4. Sofia's parents gave her an allowance for summer camp of $125. If she is going to be at camp for 6 weeks, what is the most she can spend each week while she is at camp?

Let *m* represent the amount Sofia can spend each week.

Inequality: _____

The most Sofia can spend each week is _____.

4.

5. The cell phone company allows all users 450 text messages a month. Any text messages over the allowed amount are charged $0.25 per message. Craig only has $26 extra to spend on his cell phone bill. How many messages can he go over the allowed amount for the month without breaking his budget of $26?

Let *p* represent the amount of text messages Craig can go over.

Inequality: _____

Craig can send and receive _____ extra text messages without breaking his budget of $26.

5.

Check What You Learned

Expressions, Equations, and Inequalities

Rewrite each expression using the property indicated.

a	b
1. commutative: 4×5	distributive: $6 \times (8 - 5)$
_____	_____
2. associative: $(12 \times 7) \times 8$	associative: $(3 + 4) + 5$
_____	_____
3. identity: 32×1	zero: 0×4
_____	_____

Write each phrase as an expression or equation.

4. seven less than a number

_____

eight more than a number

_____

5. the product of six and a number

_____

a number divided by twelve

_____

6. the product of 4 and a number is 16

_____

nine more than a number is 11

_____

7. three less than a number is twenty

_____

twenty-five divided by a number is five

_____

8. a number divided by 10 is 11

_____

the product of 5 and a number is 25

_____

9. 12 more than a number

_____

thirty-two divided by a number is 16

_____

10. fifteen less than a number

_____

14 divided by a number is two

_____

Check What You Learned

Expressions, Equations, and Inequalities

Solve each problem by creating an equation or inequality.

11. Yael bought two magazines for $5 and some erasers that cost $1.00 each. He could only spend $25. How many erasers could he buy?

Let *e* represent the number of erasers he was able to buy.

Equation or Inequality: _____

Yael can buy _____ erasers.

11.

12. The sum of three consecutive numbers is 75. What is the smallest of these numbers?

Let *n* represent the smallest number.

Equation or Inequality: _____

_____ is the smallest number in the set.

12.

13. Summer won 40 super bouncy balls playing Skee Ball at her school's fall festival. Later, she gave 3 to each of her friends. She only has 7 remaining. How many friends does she have?

Let *f* represent the number of friends.

Equation or Inequality: _____

Summer shared with _____ friends.

13.

14. Mrs. Watson had some candy to give to her students. She first took ten pieces for herself and then evenly divided the rest among her students. Each student received two pieces. If she started with 50 pieces of candy, how many students does she teach?

Let *s* represent the number of students.

Equation or Inequality: _____

Mrs. Watson teaches _____ students.

14.

15. The Cooking Club made some cakes to sell at a baseball game to raise money for the school library. The cafeteria contributed 5 cakes to the sale. Each cake was then cut into 10 pieces and sold. There were a total of 80 pieces to sell. How many cakes did the club make?

Let *c* represent the number of cakes.

Equation or Inequality: _____

The club made _____ cakes.

15.

NAME _____

Check What You Know

Ratios and Proportional Relationships

Solve each proportion.

a   b   c

1. $\frac{8}{15} = \frac{24}{n}$ __45__ $\frac{3}{6} = \frac{n}{2}$ __1__ $\frac{7}{n} = \frac{14}{16}$ _____

2. $\frac{8}{n} = \frac{1}{3}$ __24__ $\frac{n}{10} = \frac{4}{8}$ _____ $\frac{6}{n} = \frac{16}{24}$ _____

Circle the ratios that are equal. Show your work.

3. $\frac{3}{9}, \frac{1}{3}$ $\frac{6}{18}, \frac{2}{6}$ $\frac{1}{2}, \frac{1}{4}$

Find the constant of proportionality for each set of values.

a

4.

x	1	2	3	4
y	2	4	6	8

b

x	3	6	9	12
y	1	2	3	4

k = _____   k = _____

Find the constant of proportionality.

5.
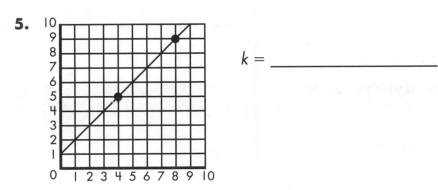

k = _____

Spectrum Math
Grade 7

Check What You Know
Chapter 4
53

Check What You Know

SHOW YOUR WORK

Ratios and Proportional Relationships

Solve each problem.

6. Three baskets of oranges weigh 120 pounds. How many pounds are in 4 baskets?

There are _____ 160 _____ pounds in 4 baskets.

6. $120 \div 3 = 40$
$40 \times 4 = 160$

7. There are 60 pencils in 4 pencil boxes. How many pencils are in 7 boxes?

There are _____ 105 _____ pencils in 7 boxes.

7. $60 \div 4 = 15$
$15 \times 7 = 105$

8. The supply store sells 4 pencils for every 5 pens. The store sold 28 pencils yesterday. How many pens did it sell?

The store sold _____ 35 _____ pens.

8. $4pc \times 7 = 28 pc$
$5p \times 7 = 35p$

9. A restaurant charges an automatic 20% tip for groups of 6 or more. A group of 8 people had a bill of $187. How much was their tip?

Their tip was _____.

9.

10. A mail order company charges $4\frac{1}{2}$% for shipping and handling on all orders. If the total for an order is $54.34, how much was the order total before shipping and handling?

Let *r* stand for the order total.

Equation: _____

The order before shipping and handling

is _____ .

10.

11. Elizabeth can run 5 miles in $24\frac{1}{2}$ minutes. Dez can run 8 miles in $32\frac{1}{3}$ minutes. Who can run faster?

Let *e* represent Elizabeth's speed and *d* represent Dez's speed.

Equivalent Ratio 1: _____

Equivalent Ratio 2: _____

_____ can run faster.

11.

Lesson 4.1 Unit Rates with Fractions

A **rate** is a special ratio in which two terms are in different units. A **unit rate** is when one of those terms is expressed as a value of 1. Rates can be calculated with whole numbers or with fractions.

Emily ate $\frac{1}{4}$ of an ice-cream cone in $\frac{1}{2}$ of a minute. How long would it take her to eat one ice-cream cone?

1. Set up equivalent ratios using the information from the problem and 1 to represent the ice cream cone. Let t represent the time. $\quad \frac{\frac{1}{2}}{\frac{1}{4}} = \frac{t}{1}$

2. Use cross multiplication. $\quad \frac{1}{4} \times t = \frac{1}{2} \times 1$

3. Isolate the variable. $\quad \frac{1}{4} \times t \div \frac{1}{4} = \frac{1}{2} \times 1 \div \frac{1}{4}$

4. Solve. $\quad t = 2$

SHOW YOUR WORK

Find the unit rate in each problem.

1. For Bill's birthday his mom is bringing donuts to school. She has a coupon to get $2\frac{1}{2}$ dozen donuts for $8.00. How much would just one dozen donuts cost at this price?

   Let c represent the cost of the donuts.

   Equivalent ratios: ___$\frac{2\frac{1}{2}}{8} = \frac{d}{c}$___

   One dozen donuts would cost _____.

2. Jake ate $4\frac{1}{2}$ pounds of candy in one week. If he ate the same amount of candy every day, how much candy did he eat each day?

   Let c represent the amount of candy.

   Equivalent ratios: _____

   He ate _____ pounds of candy each day.

3. A bakery used $6\frac{1}{4}$ cups of flour this morning to make 5 batches of cookies. How much flour went into each batch of cookies?

   Let f represent the amount of flour.

   Equivalent ratios: _____

   Each batch of cookies used _____ cups of flour.

1.
$$8 \times d = 2\frac{1}{2} \times c \quad \div 8$$
$$8 \times d \div 8 = 2\frac{1}{2} \times c \div 8$$
$$d =$$

2.

3.

Lesson 4.1 Unit Rates with Fractions

Using unit rates can help you compare two items.

Mike's car can travel 425 miles on $10\frac{1}{2}$ gallons of gas. Jason's car can travel 275 miles on $5\frac{4}{5}$ gallons of gas. Which car gets better gas mileage?

Let m represent Mike's car and j represent Jason's car.

Equivalent Ratio 1: $\dfrac{425}{10\frac{1}{2}} = \dfrac{m}{1}$ $m = 40\frac{10}{21}$ miles per gallon

Equivalent Ratio 2: $\dfrac{275}{5\frac{4}{5}} = \dfrac{j}{1}$ $j = 47\frac{12}{29}$ miles per gallon

Jason's car gets better gas mileage because it can go farther on one gallon of gas.

SHOW YOUR WORK

Calculate unit rates to solve each problem.

1. Cara can run 3 miles in $27\frac{1}{2}$ minutes. Melanie can run 6 miles in $53\frac{1}{3}$ minutes. Who can run faster?

   Let c represent Cara's speed and m represent Melanie's speed.

   Equivalent Ratio 1: _____

   Equivalent Ratio 2: _____

   _____ can run faster.

   1.

2. Bob goes to Shop and Save and buys $3\frac{1}{3}$ pounds of turkey for $10.50. Sonia goes to Quick Stop and buys $2\frac{1}{2}$ pounds of turkey for $6.25. Who got a better deal?

   Let b represent Bob's price and s represent Sonia's price.

   Equivalent Ratio 1: _____

   Equivalent Ratio 2: _____

   _____ got a better deal on turkey.

   2.

3. Thomas went for a long hike and burned 675 calories in $2\frac{1}{2}$ hours. Marvin decided to go for a bike ride and burned 1,035 calories in $3\frac{1}{4}$ hours. Who burned the most calories per hour?

   Let t represent Thomas's calories burned and m represent Marvin's calories burned.

   Equivalent Ratio 1: _____

   Equivalent Ratio 2: _____

   _____ burned the most calories per hour.

   3.

Lesson 4.2 Testing Proportional Relationships

Relationships are proportional if they indicate the relationship between values stays constant. Graphing values can help determine if the relationship is proportional.

x	2	4	6	8	10
y	3	6	9	12	15

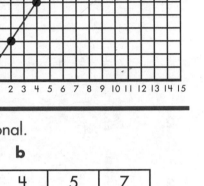

Step 1: Graph each point on a grid.

Step 2: Connect the points.

Step 3: Decide if the line is straight or not.

If the line connecting points on a grid is straight, the relationship between the quantities is proportional.

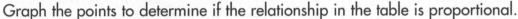

Graph the points to determine if the relationship in the table is proportional.

a

1.
x	7.5	10	17.5	20
y	4.5	6	10.5	12

b

x	2	4	5	7
y	1	3	2.5	3.5

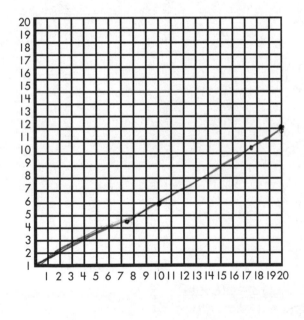

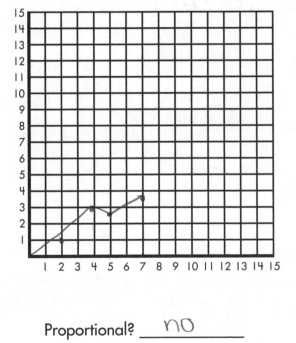

Proportional? ___yes___

Proportional? ___no___

NAME _____

Lesson 4.2 Testing Proportional Relationships

A **ratio** is a comparison of two numbers. A **proportion** expresses the equality of two ratios.

A ratio can be expressed as 1 to 2, 1:2, or $\frac{1}{2}$, and it means that for every 1 of the first item, there are 2 of the other item.

Cross-multiply to determine if two ratios are equal.

$\frac{2}{4}, \frac{3}{6}$ $2 \times 6 = 12$ $3 \times 4 = 12$ $\frac{2}{4} = \frac{3}{6}$

Circle the ratios that are equal. Show your work.

	a	**b**	**c**
1.	$\frac{1}{3}, \frac{2}{6}$	$\frac{3}{8}, \frac{1}{4}$	$\frac{3}{5}, \frac{9}{15}$
2.	$\frac{3}{4}, \frac{9}{12}$	$\frac{1}{2}, \frac{4}{8}$	$\frac{5}{6}, \frac{15}{18}$
3.	$\frac{5}{8}, \frac{4}{7}$	$\frac{1}{2}, \frac{1}{4}$	$\frac{4}{3}, \frac{16}{12}$
4.	$\frac{6}{18}, \frac{2}{6}$	$\frac{3}{25}, \frac{6}{50}$	$\frac{1}{8}, \frac{2}{10}$
5.	$\frac{1}{4}, \frac{2}{4}$	$\frac{5}{10}, \frac{3}{6}$	$\frac{4}{24}, \frac{7}{42}$
6.	$\frac{3}{5}, \frac{5}{3}$	$\frac{7}{8}, \frac{21}{24}$	$\frac{8}{23}, \frac{9}{46}$
7.	$\frac{7}{4}, \frac{28}{16}$	$\frac{3}{9}, \frac{1}{3}$	$\frac{16}{20}, \frac{9}{10}$
8.	$\frac{8}{100}, \frac{80}{50}$	$\frac{8}{12}, \frac{10}{14}$	$\frac{15}{20}, \frac{3}{4}$
9.	$\frac{9}{2}, \frac{12}{3}$	$\frac{6}{3}, \frac{8}{4}$	$\frac{1}{3}, \frac{11}{33}$
10.	$\frac{12}{7}, \frac{36}{21}$	$\frac{10}{12}, \frac{15}{20}$	$\frac{3}{4}, \frac{9}{16}$

Lesson 4.2 Testing Proportional Relationships

Cross-multiply to check each proportion. Circle the ratios that are true.

	a	**b**	**c**

1. $\frac{4}{3} = \frac{6}{4}$ _____ $\frac{1}{4} = \frac{3}{12}$ _____ $\frac{4}{5} = \frac{16}{20}$ _____

2. $\frac{8}{12} = \frac{2}{3}$ _____ $\frac{30}{25} = \frac{6}{5}$ _____ $\frac{7}{3} = \frac{5}{2}$ _____

3. $\frac{9}{1} = \frac{18}{3}$ _____ $\frac{15}{4} = \frac{45}{12}$ _____ $\frac{2}{5} = \frac{4}{12}$ _____

4. $\frac{7}{4} = \frac{21}{12}$ _____ $\frac{9}{2} = \frac{18}{6}$ _____ $\frac{5}{6} = \frac{15}{18}$ _____

5. $\frac{5}{9} = \frac{10}{19}$ _____ $\frac{4}{3} = \frac{16}{12}$ _____ $\frac{7}{4} = \frac{14}{10}$ _____

6. $\frac{12}{8} = \frac{18}{12}$ _____ $\frac{14}{7} = \frac{6}{3}$ _____ $\frac{1}{5} = \frac{3}{16}$ _____

7. $\frac{2}{1} = \frac{6}{2}$ _____ $\frac{8}{6} = \frac{12}{8}$ _____ $\frac{5}{4} = \frac{10}{8}$ _____

8. $\frac{2}{5} = \frac{6}{15}$ _____ $\frac{14}{6} = \frac{21}{8}$ _____ $\frac{4}{5} = \frac{10}{16}$ _____

9. $\frac{3}{5} = \frac{9}{20}$ _____ $\frac{1}{3} = \frac{4}{12}$ _____ $\frac{9}{6} = \frac{12}{8}$ _____

10. $\frac{7}{5} = \frac{28}{20}$ _____ $\frac{5}{4} = \frac{25}{16}$ _____ $\frac{10}{13} = \frac{30}{26}$ _____

11. $\frac{4}{5} = \frac{20}{22}$ _____ $\frac{1}{5} = \frac{3}{18}$ _____ $\frac{6}{7} = \frac{78}{91}$ _____

12. $\frac{2}{9} = \frac{30}{135}$ _____ $\frac{8}{3} = \frac{96}{36}$ _____ $\frac{5}{2} = \frac{75}{20}$ _____

Lesson 4.3 Constants of Proportionality

A unit rate can also be called a **constant of proportionality**. The constant of proportionality describes the rate at which variables in an equation change.

x	2	3	5	6
y	6	9	15	18

Step 1: Set up an equation in which the constant (k) is equal to $y \div x$.

Step 2: Check the equation across multiple points to verify the constant.

Step 3: $6 \div 2 = 3$; $9 \div 3 = 3$; $15 \div 5 = 3$; $k = 3$

Find the constant of proportionality for each set of values.

a

b

1.

x	1	2	3	8
y	1.5	3	4.5	12

x	0.4	0.8	1.4	1.8
y	2	4	7	9

$k =$ _____

$k =$ _____

2.

x	1	2	2.5	3.5
y	2	4	5	7

x	4.5	6	10.5	12
y	7.5	10	17.5	20

$k =$ _____

$k =$ _____

3.

x	2	4	6	8
y	1	2	3	4

x	10	20	30	40
y	2	4	6	8

$k =$ _____

$k =$ _____

Lesson 4.3 Constants of Proportionality

Find the constant of proportionality for each set of values.

	a			

1.

x	1	2	3	4
y	2	4	6	8

x	3	6	9	12
y	2	4	6	8

k = _____   k = _____

2.

x	5	15	25	35
y	1	3	5	7

x	5	10	15	25
y	4	8	12	20

k = _____   k = _____

3.

x	18	30	42	54
y	3	5	7	9

x	0.25	1	3	4
y	0.5	2	6	8

k = _____   k = _____

4.

x	4	8	12	16
y	1	2	3	4

x	4	8	12	16
y	3	6	9	12

k = _____   k = _____

Lesson 4.4 Using Equations to Represent Proportions

Sometimes words are used to describe the proportional relationship in a problem. The words can tell how to write an equation to represent a proportional relationship.

A handicapped-access ramp starts at ground level and rises to 27 inches over a distance of 30 feet. What is the equation to find the height of the ramp based on how far along the ramp you have traveled?

1. Use the equation to find the constant of proportionality: $k = \frac{y}{x}$. For simplicity, use the known value (27) of the variable you will be solving for (height) as y when setting up the proportion.

2. In this problem, $k = \frac{27}{30}$, where 27 is the height of the ramp (y) and 30 is the distance it covers (x).

3. Simplify to $k = \frac{9}{10}$. This is the constant of proportionality for this problem, so you can plug this value into the equation in step 1 to get $\frac{9}{10} = \frac{y}{x}$.

4. With this proportion, you can find the height at any point along the ramp. Just isolate the variable you are solving for (x, or height) on one side of the equation. So, $y = \frac{9}{10} \times x$.

SHOW YOUR WORK

Write the equation to solve each problem. Use y as the variable you solve for.

1. A recipe to make 4 pancakes calls for 6 tablespoons of flour. Tracy wants to make 10 pancakes using this recipe. What equation will she need to use to find out how many tablespoons of flour to use?

   Equation: _____

   1.

2. A picture measures 11 inches tall by 14 inches wide. Nathan wants to enlarge the picture to fit in a frame that is 16 inches wide. What equation will he need to use to find out how wide the picture should be after it is enlarged?

   Equation: _____

   2.

3. A car uses 8 gallons of gasoline to travel 290 miles. Juanita wants to take a trip that is 400 miles. What equation will she need to use to find out how much gas the trip will use?

   Equation: _____

   3.

4. After Marco has worked for 5 hours, he has earned $29.00. He is planning to work 30 hours this week. What equation will he need to use to find out how much he will be paid?

   Equation: _____

   4.

Lesson 4.4 Problem Solving

Write the equation to solve each problem. Use *x* as the variable you solve for.

1. Chester wants to plant a flower bed that is 80 square feet. Each packet of seeds gives him enough flowers to cover 10 square feet of the flower bed. What equation will he use to find out how many packets of seeds to buy for his flower bed?

Equation: _____

2. At the Charming Chair Factory, they make 20 chairs per day when 5 workers are on duty. If they need to make 100 chairs in one day, what equation should they use to figure out how many workers to schedule?

Equation: _____

3. Henry is an artist who can produce 5 paintings every 2 months. He is getting ready for an exhibit and has to make 8 new paintings. What equation should he use to figure out how long it will take him to get his paintings ready?

Equation: _____

4. Andrea rents a bike for 8 hours and pays $42.00 for the rental. Tomorrow, she wants to rent the same bike, but only needs it for 6 hours. What equation can she use to figure out how much she will need to pay?

Equation: _____

5. Sara can bake 12 cookies with 2 scoops of flour. If she wants to make 36 cookies, what equation should she use to help her find out how many scoops of flour to use?

Equation: _____

1.

2.

3.

4.

5.

Lesson 4.5 Proportional Relationships on the Coordinate Plane

When proportional relationships are graphed, the points the line runs through can be used to find the constant of proportionality.

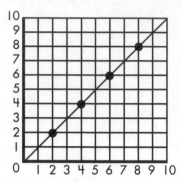

This line runs through points (2, 2), (4, 4), (6, 6), and (8, 8).

First, find the proportion of this relationship by choosing one point and inserting its coordinates into the proportion equation.

$$k = \frac{y_2 - y_1}{x_2 - x_1} \quad \text{or} \quad k = \frac{4 - 2}{4 - 2} = \frac{2}{2} = 1$$

The constant of proportionality for this line is 1.

Find the constant of proportionality for each graph.

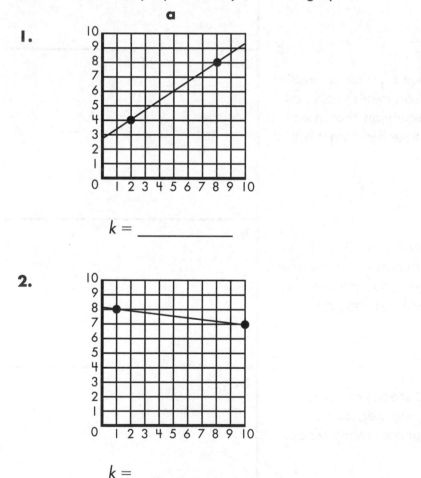

a

1.

$k =$ _____

b

$k =$ _____

2.

$k =$ _____

$k =$ _____

Lesson 4.5 Proportional Relationships on the Coordinate Plane

Find the constant of proportionality for each graph.

a   **b**

1.

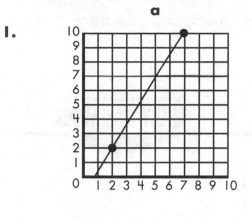

$k =$ _____

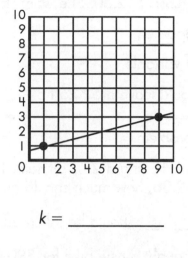

$k =$ _____

2.

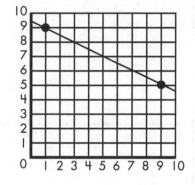

$k =$ _____

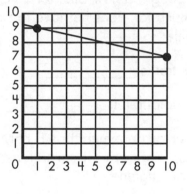

$k =$ _____

3.

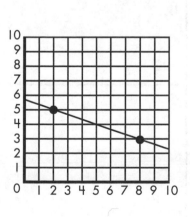

$k =$ _____

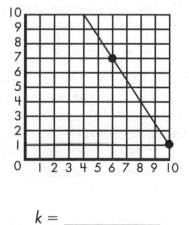

$k =$ _____

Lesson 4.6 Problem Solving

Proportional relationships can be used to solve ratio and percent problems.

Mika's lunch costs $12.50. She wants to leave an 18% tip. How much should she leave?

Set up a proportion. $\frac{x}{12.50} = \frac{18}{100}$

Solve for the variable. $225 = 100x$

So, Mika should leave a $2.25 tip. $2.25 = x$

SHOW YOUR WORK

Solve each problem.

1. A store is having a 25% off sale. If an item originally cost $19.36, how much should be taken off the price?

   _____ should be taken off the original price.

   1.

2. Dario bought a new bike for $90.00. Sales tax is $5\frac{1}{2}$%. How much tax does he have to pay? How much is his total bill?

   Dario's tax is _____.

   Dario's total bill is _____.

   2.

3. A flower arrangement has 8 carnations for every 4 roses. There are 14 carnations. How many roses are in the arrangement?

   There are _____ roses in the arrangement.

   3.

4. There are 18 girls in the school choir. The ratio of girls to boys is 1 to 2. How many boys are in the choir?

   There are _____ boys in the choir.

   4.

5. A baseball player strikes out 3 times for every 2 hits he gets. If the player strikes out 15 times, how many hits does he get? If the player gets 46 hits, how many times does he strike out?

   The player gets _____ hits for every 15 times he strikes out.

   If the player gets 46 hits, he strikes out _____ times.

   5.

Lesson 4.6 Problem Solving

SHOW YOUR WORK

Solve each problem.

1. Mr. Johnson borrowed $750 for 1 year. He has to pay 6% simple interest. How much interest will he pay?

   Mr. Johnson will pay _____ in interest.

2. Mrs. Soto invested in a certificate of deposit that pays 8% interest. Her investment was $325. How much interest will she receive in 1 year?

   Mrs. Soto will receive _____ in interest.

3. Andrea put $52 in a savings account that pays 4% interest. How much interest will she earn in 1 year?

   Andrea will earn _____ in interest.

4. Jonas purchased a 42-month ($3\frac{1}{2}$ year) certificate of deposit. It cost $600 and pays 7% interest each year. How much interest will he get? How much will the certificate be worth when he cashes it in?

   Jonas will get _____ in interest.

   The certificate will be worth _____.

5. Rick borrowed $50 from his sister for 3 months ($\frac{1}{4}$ year). She charged him 14% interest. How much does Rick have to pay to his sister?

   Rick must pay his sister a total of _____.

6. The grocery store borrowed $15,000 to remodel. The term is 7 years and the yearly interest rate is $4\frac{1}{4}$%. How much interest will the store pay? What is the total amount to be repaid?

   The store will pay _____ in interest.

   The total amount to be repaid is _____.

1.

2.

3.

4.

5.

6.

Check What You Learned

Ratios and Proportional Relationships

Solve each proportion.

      a   **b**   **c**

1. $\frac{3}{2} = \frac{n}{6}$ _____ $\frac{17}{34} = \frac{1}{n}$ _____ $\frac{n}{16} = \frac{6}{4}$ _____

2. $\frac{7}{n} = \frac{21}{12}$ _____ $\frac{5}{8} = \frac{n}{40}$ _____ $\frac{1}{2} = \frac{56}{n}$ _____

Circle the ratios that are equal. Show your work.

3. $\frac{15}{20}, \frac{3}{4}$ $\frac{8}{12}, \frac{10}{14}$ $\frac{4}{3}, \frac{16}{12}$

Find the constant of proportionality for each set of values.

            a   **b**

4.

x	1	2	3	4
y	5	10	15	20

x	2	4	6	8
y	10	20	30	40

     $k =$ _____ $k =$ _____

Find the constant of proportionality.

5.

$k =$ _____

Check What You Learned

SHOW YOUR WORK

Ratios and Proportional Relationships

Solve each problem.

6. Lisa ran $3\frac{1}{2}$ miles in 21 minutes. At that rate, how long would it take her to run 5 miles?

It would take Lisa _____ minutes to run 5 miles.

6.

7. Manuel biked $12\frac{1}{4}$ miles in 45 minutes. At that rate, how far could he go in 1 hour?

Manuel could bike _____ miles in 1 hour.

7.

8. A recipe to make 5 cupcakes calls for 10 tablespoons of sugar. Alicia wants to make 10 cupcakes using this recipe. What equation will she need to use to find out how many tablespoons of sugar to use?

Equation: _____

8.

9. Luis has $660 in his savings account earning $4\frac{1}{2}$ % interest. How much interest will he earn in 2 years? How much money will be in the account?

Luis will earn _____ in interest.

He will have a total of _____ in his account.

9.

10. Mrs. Cole borrowed $1,200 for 6 months ($\frac{1}{2}$ year) at $3\frac{1}{4}$ % interest. How much interest will she pay? What is the total amount she will pay?

Mrs. Cole will pay _____ in interest.

She will pay a total of _____.

10.

11. Flo worked for 9 hours and has earned $108.00. She is planning to work 40 hours this week. What equation will she need to use to find out how much she will be paid?

Equation: _____

11.

12. Ansley went for a long hike and burned 452 calories in $2\frac{1}{4}$ hours. Bobbi decided to go for a jog and burned 1,045 calories in $3\frac{1}{2}$ hours. Who burned the most calories per hour?

Let *a* represent Ansley's and *b* represent Bobbi's calories burned.

Equivalent Ratio 1: _____

Equivalent Ratio 2: _____

_____ burned the most calories per hour.

12.

Mid-Test Chapters 1–4

Add, subtract, multiply, or divide. Write each answer in simplest form.

   a   **b**   **c**   **d**

1. $\frac{5}{6} + \frac{1}{6} =$ _____ $\frac{3}{4} + \frac{2}{3} =$ _____ $4\frac{2}{3} + 3\frac{1}{4} =$ _____ $2\frac{1}{6} + 2\frac{1}{3} =$ _____

2. $\frac{7}{8} - \frac{5}{8} =$ _____ $\frac{5}{6} - \frac{2}{3} =$ _____ $5\frac{3}{4} - 2\frac{2}{3} =$ _____ $6\frac{1}{2} - 3\frac{5}{6} =$ _____

3. $\frac{1}{4} \times \frac{5}{6} =$ _____ $\frac{3}{8} \times \frac{2}{3} =$ _____ $2\frac{5}{7} \times \frac{4}{9} =$ _____ $\frac{1}{2} \times \frac{3}{5} \times \frac{1}{8} =$ _____

4. $\frac{2}{3} \div \frac{4}{7} =$ _____ $3\frac{1}{2} \div \frac{5}{6} =$ _____ $\frac{4}{9} \div \frac{1}{12} =$ _____ $2\frac{2}{3} \div 1\frac{1}{8} =$ _____

5. $(-12) + 7 =$ _____ $(-10) + (-7) =$ _____ $(-6) + 12 =$ _____ $8 + 7 =$ _____

6. $3 + 4 =$ _____ $(-45) + 9 =$ _____ $(-1) + (-46) =$ _____ $(-30) + 10 =$ _____

7. $0 - 6 =$ _____ $(-4) - 3 =$ _____ $9 - (-8) =$ _____ $(-5) - 1 =$ _____

8. $9 - 2 =$ _____ $3 - 6 =$ _____ $8 - (-3) =$ _____ $(-3) - 9 =$ _____

Mid-Test Chapters 1–4

Multiply or divide.

	a	b	c	d
9.	$6 \times (-4) =$ _____	$4 \times 2 =$ _____	$(-6) \times 5 =$ _____	$(-6) \times (-10) =$ _____
10.	$35 \div (-5) =$ _____	$(-8) \div 4 =$ _____	$(-24) \div 4 =$ _____	$(-8) \div (-2) =$ _____

Change each rational number into a decimal.

	a	b	c
11.	$\frac{3}{5} =$ _____	$\frac{7}{50} =$ _____	$\frac{1}{111} =$ _____

Evaluate the following expressions.

	a	b	c	d
12.	$|-5| =$ _____	$-|46| =$ _____	$|-3| =$ _____	$|32| =$ _____

Write *yes* or *no* to tell if each set of ratios is proportional.

13. $\frac{5}{6}, \frac{7}{8}$ _____ $\frac{4}{5}, \frac{12}{15}$ _____ $\frac{6}{7}, \frac{12}{14}$ _____ $\frac{1}{3}, \frac{2}{5}$ _____

14. $\frac{7}{8}, \frac{14}{16}$ _____ $\frac{3}{4}, \frac{9}{12}$ _____ $\frac{9}{10}, \frac{27}{30}$ _____ $\frac{2}{3}, \frac{16}{25}$ _____

Write the name of the property shown by each equation.

	a	b	c
	15. $42 + 0 = 42$	$(7 \times 2) \times 5 = 7 \times (2 \times 5)$	$2 + 6 = 6 + 2$
	_____	_____	_____

Mid-Test Chapters 1–4

Find the constant of proportionality for each set of values.

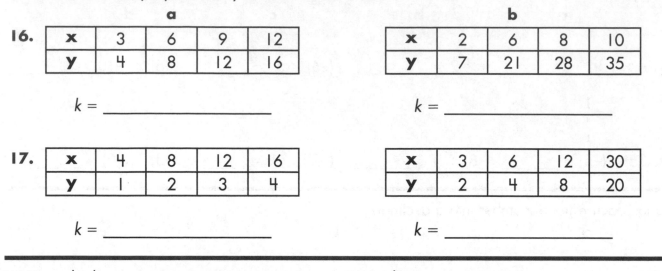

	a			
x	3	6	9	12
y	4	8	12	16

16.

k = _____

	b			
x	2	6	8	10
y	7	21	28	35

k = _____

x	4	8	12	16
y	1	2	3	4

17.

k = _____

x	3	6	12	30
y	2	4	8	20

k = _____

Write each phrase as an expression, equation, or inequality.

18. six times a number is greater than 12   the product of three and the opposite of 4

_____   _____

19. the sum of 2 and the quotient of 45 and 9   the difference between 4 and 9

_____   _____

Solve each inequality and graph its solution.

20. $j \div 4 < -18$ $-5k \geq -20$

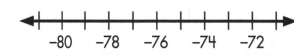

CHAPTERS 1–4 MID-TEST

Mid-Test Chapters 1–4

Solve each problem.

21. A can of mixed nuts has 5 peanuts for every 2 cashews. There are 175 peanuts in the can. How many cashews are there?

There are _____ cashews in the can.

21.

22. A savings account pays $4\frac{1}{2}$ % interest. How much interest will be earned on $450 in 3 years? How much money will be in the account in 3 years?

The account will earn _____ in interest in 3 years.

There will be _____ in the account in 3 years.

22.

23. The Kendalls make monthly deposits into their savings plan. In 7 months, they have deposited $224. If they continue at this rate, how much will they have deposited in 12 months?

The will have deposited _____.

23.

24. For a field trip, 6 students rode in cars and the rest filled 8 buses. How many students were in each bus if 326 students were on the trip?

Let s represent the number of students on each bus.

Equation: _____

There were _____ students on each bus.

24.

Graph the points to determine if the relationship in the table is proportional.

25.

x	4	6	2	7
y	1	3	4	8

Proportional? _____

Find the constant of proportionality.

26.

$k =$ _____

NAME _____

Check What You Know

Geometry

Find the area of each figure.

a	b	c

1.

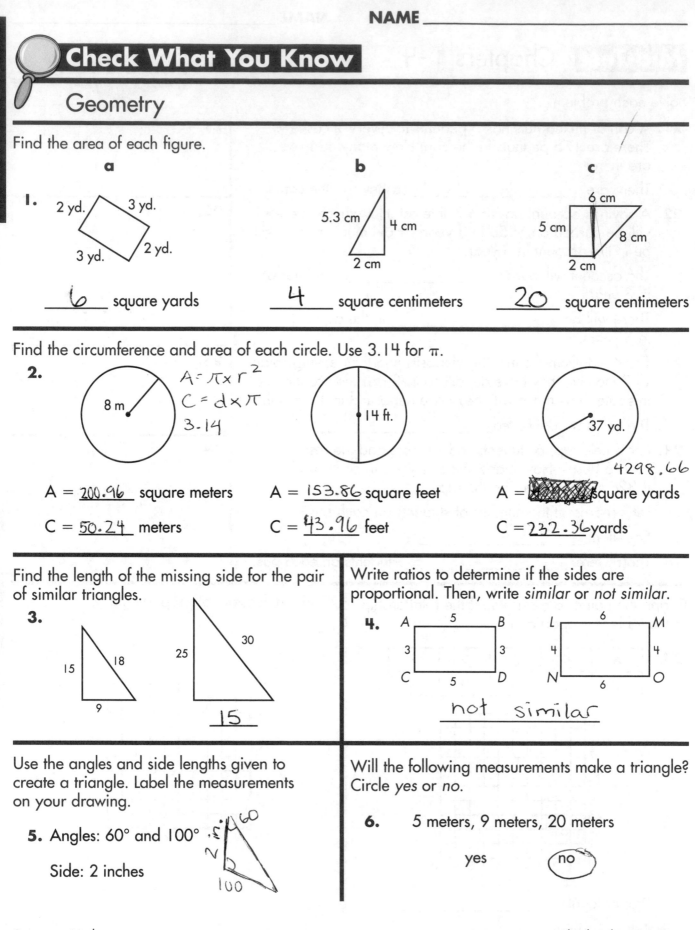

2 yd.   3 yd.
3 yd.   2 yd.

___6___ square yards

5.3 cm   4 cm
2 cm

___4___ square centimeters

6 cm
5 cm   8 cm
2 cm

___20___ square centimeters

Find the circumference and area of each circle. Use 3.14 for π.

2.

8 m

$A = \pi \times r^2$
$C = d \times \pi$
3.14

14 ft.

37 yd.

4298.66

A = __200.96__ square meters

A = __153.86__ square feet

A = ~~XXXXX~~ square yards

C = __50.24__ meters

C = __43.96__ feet

C = __232.36__ yards

Find the length of the missing side for the pair of similar triangles.

3.

15   18
9

25   30
__15__

Write ratios to determine if the sides are proportional. Then, write *similar* or *not similar*.

4.

A —5— B
3   3
C —5— D

L —6— M
4   4
N —6— O

__not similar__

Use the angles and side lengths given to create a triangle. Label the measurements on your drawing.

5. Angles: 60° and 100°

Side: 2 inches

2 in. 60
100

Will the following measurements make a triangle? Circle *yes* or *no*.

6.   5 meters, 9 meters, 20 meters

yes   (no)

Check What You Know

Geometry

Find the volume of each figure.

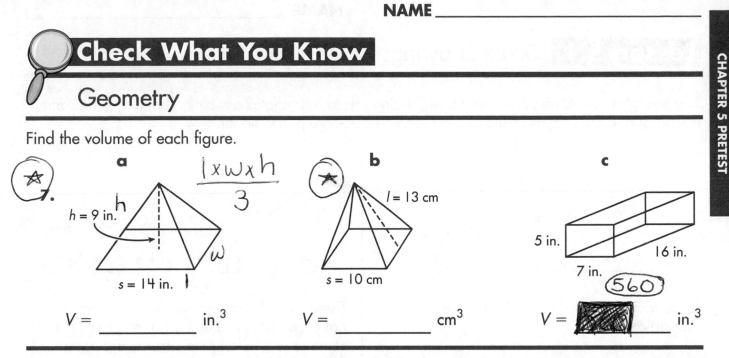

a

$\dfrac{l \times w \times h}{3}$

⭐ **7.**

$h = 9$ in.

$s = 14$ in.

$V =$ _____ in.^{3}

b

⭐

$l = 13$ cm

$s = 10$ cm

$V =$ _____ cm^3

c

5 in.

16 in.

7 in.

(560)

$V =$ ⬛ in.^{3}

Tell what shape is created by each cross section.

Use the figure below to answer the questions.

8.

<u>square</u>

9.

<u>quadrilateral</u>

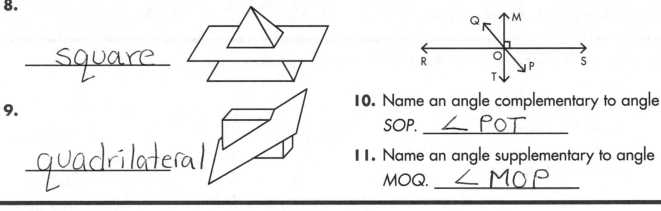

10. Name an angle complementary to angle SOP. <u>∠ POT</u>

11. Name an angle supplementary to angle MOQ. <u>∠ MOP</u>

Solve each problem.

12. A scale drawing of a car is 3 inches to 12 inches. If the car is 48 inches high, how high is the drawing?

The drawing is <u>12</u> inches high.

13. On a map, each inch represents 25 miles. What is the length of a highway if it is 6 inches long on a map?

The highway is <u>150</u> miles long.

14. Adam needs to wrap a package that is 11 inches long, 8.5 inches wide, and 6 inches high. What is the volume of the package?

The package's volume is <u>561</u> cubic inches.

12.

13.

14.

Lesson 5.1 Scale Drawings

Two triangles are **similar** if their corresponding (matching) angles are congruent (have the same measure) and the lengths of their corresponding sides are proportional.

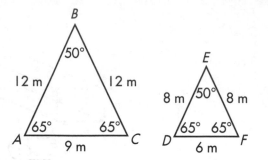

These triangles are similar. All the sides are proportional.

$$\frac{AB}{DE} = \frac{12}{8} = \frac{3}{2} \qquad \frac{BC}{EF} = \frac{12}{8} = \frac{3}{2} \qquad \frac{AC}{DF} = \frac{9}{6} = \frac{3}{2}$$

The angle measures are congruent.

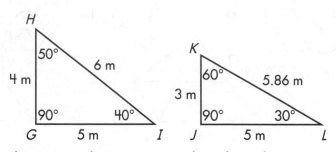

These triangles are not similar. The sides are not proportional. They do not all create the same ratio. The angle measures are not all congruent.

$$\frac{GH}{JK} = \frac{4}{3} \qquad \frac{HI}{KL} = \frac{6}{5.86} \qquad \frac{GI}{JL} = \frac{5}{5} = \frac{1}{1}$$

For each pair of triangles, check that their sides are proportional. Circle *similar* or *not similar*.

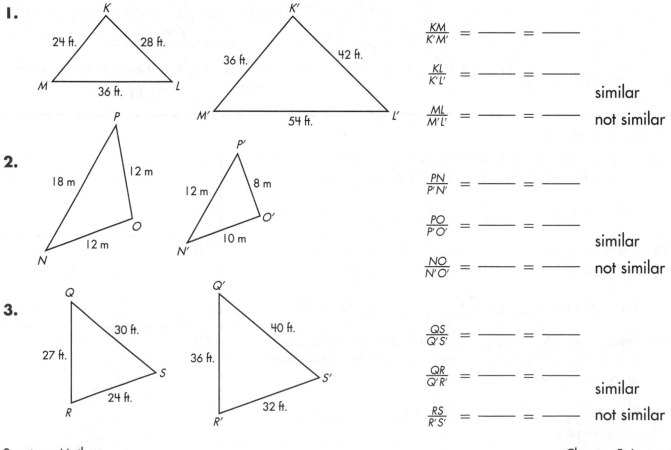

1.

$\dfrac{KM}{K'M'} = $ _____ = _____

$\dfrac{KL}{K'L'} = $ _____ = _____

$\dfrac{ML}{M'L'} = $ _____ = _____

similar

not similar

2.

$\dfrac{PN}{P'N'} = $ _____ = _____

$\dfrac{PO}{P'O'} = $ _____ = _____

$\dfrac{NO}{N'O'} = $ _____ = _____

similar

not similar

3.

$\dfrac{QS}{Q'S'} = $ _____ = _____

$\dfrac{QR}{Q'R'} = $ _____ = _____

$\dfrac{RS}{R'S'} = $ _____ = _____

similar

not similar

Lesson 5.1 Scale Drawings

When you know that two triangles are similar, you can use the ratio of the known lengths of the sides to figure the unknown length.

What is the length of *EF*?

$\dfrac{AC}{DF} = \dfrac{BC}{EF}$ $\dfrac{4}{6} = \dfrac{12}{n}$ Use a proportion.

$4n = 72$ $n = 18$ Cross multiply.

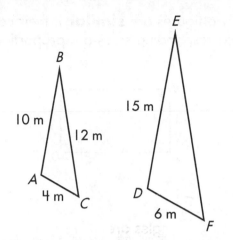

Find the length of the missing side for each pair of similar triangles. Label the side with its length.

a   **b**

1.

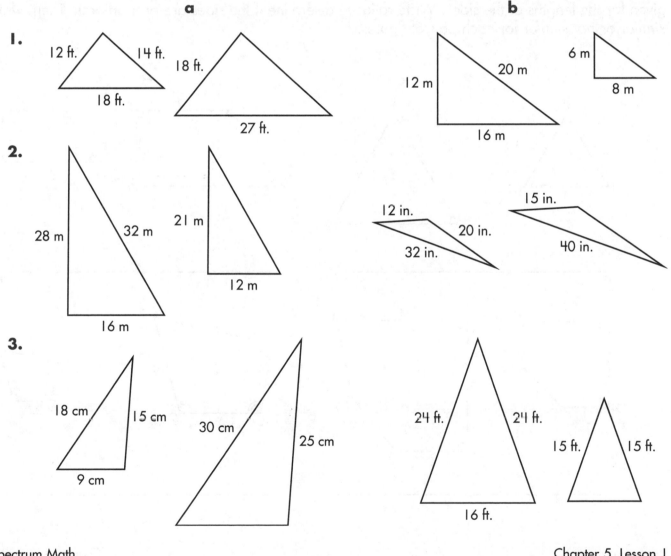

Lesson 5.1 Scale Drawings

Two figures are **similar** if their corresponding angles are congruent and the lengths of their corresponding sides are proportional. Write a ratio to determine if the sides are proportional.

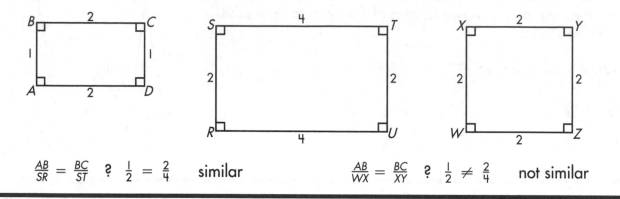

$\frac{AB}{SR} = \frac{BC}{ST}$? $\frac{1}{2} = \frac{2}{4}$ similar $\frac{AB}{WX} = \frac{BC}{XY}$? $\frac{1}{2} \neq \frac{2}{4}$ not similar

In the following figures, the angle marks indicate which angles are congruent. Use the measures given for the lengths of the sides. Write ratios to determine if the sides are proportional. Then, write *similar* or *not similar* for each pair of figures.

a   **b**

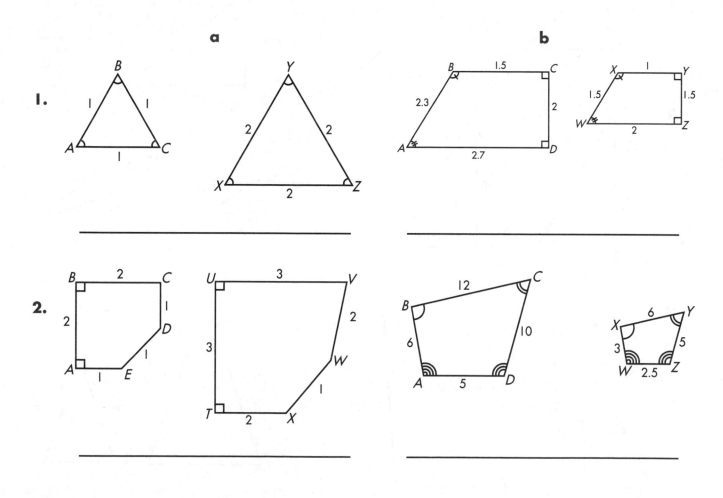

1.

_____   _____

2.

_____   _____

Lesson 5.2 Problem Solving

A **scale drawing** is a drawing of a real object in which all of the dimensions are proportional to the real object. A scale drawing can be larger or smaller than the object it represents. The **scale** is the ratio of the drawing size to the actual size of the object.

A drawing of a person has a scale of 2 inches = 1 foot. If the drawing is 11 inches high, how tall is the person?

$$\frac{2}{1} = \frac{11}{n}$$ Write a proportion.

$$\frac{1 \times 11}{2} = n$$ Solve for n.

$$5\frac{1}{2} = n$$ The person is $5\frac{1}{2}$ feet tall.

SHOW YOUR WORK

Solve each problem. Write a proportion in the space to the right.

1. A bridge is 440 yards long. A scale drawing has a ratio of 1 inch = 1 yard. How long is the drawing?

   The drawing is _____ inches long.

   1.

2. A map of the county uses a scale of 2 inches = 19 miles. If the county is 76 miles wide, how wide is the map?

   The map is _____ inches wide.

   2.

3. A picture of a goldfish has a scale of 8 centimeters to 3 centimeters. If the actual goldfish is 12 centimeters long, how long is the drawing?

   The drawing is _____ centimeters long.

   3.

4. An architect made a scale drawing of a house to be built. The scale is 2 inches to 3 feet. The house in the drawing is 24 inches tall. How tall is the actual house?

   The actual house is _____ feet tall.

   4.

Lesson 5.2 Problem Solving

SHOW YOUR WORK

Solve each problem. Write a proportion in the space to the right.

1. On an architect's blueprint, the front of a building measures 27 inches. The scale of the blueprint is 1 inch = 2 feet. How wide will the front of the actual building be?

   The building will be _____ feet wide.

2. The model of an airplane has a wingspan of 20 inches. The model has a scale of 1 inch = 4 feet. What is the wingspan of the actual airplane?

   The wingspan is _____ feet.

3. A picture of a car uses a scale of 1 inch = $\frac{1}{2}$ foot. The actual car is $8\frac{1}{2}$ feet wide. How wide will the drawing of the car be?

   The drawing will be _____ inches wide.

4. On a map, two cities are $4\frac{1}{4}$ inches apart. The scale of the map is $\frac{1}{2}$ inch = 3 miles. What is the actual distance between the towns?

   The actual distance is _____ miles.

5. Marisa is making a scale drawing of her house. Her house is 49 feet wide. On her drawing, the house is 7 inches wide. What is the scale of Marisa's drawing?

   The scale is _____.

6. The bed of Jeff's pick-up truck is 8 feet long. On a scale model of his truck, the bed is 10 inches long. What is the scale of the model?

   The scale is _____.

1.

2.

3.

4.

5.

6.

Lesson 5.3 Drawing Geometric Shapes: Triangles

When given two angle measures and one side length, a protractor and ruler can be used to create a triangle.

Draw a triangle that has angles of 30° and 80° and a side between them of two inches.

Step 1: Use a ruler to draw a line that is 2 inches.

Step 2: Use a protractor to draw a line that creates the desired angle with the first line (30°).

Step 3: Use the protractor to measure the 2nd known angle from the other end of your original line.

Step 4: Label the triangle.

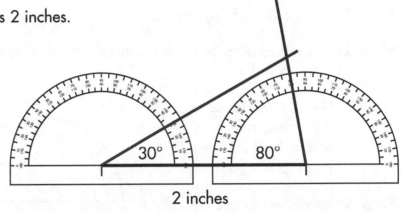

2 inches

Use the angles and side lengths given to create triangles. Label the measurements on your drawing.

	a	**b**
1.	angles: 50° and 55° side: 1 inch	angles: 120° and 30° side: 2 cm
2.	angles: 75° and 40° side: 3 inches	angles: 60° and 100° side: 2 inches

Lesson 5.3 Drawing Geometric Shapes: Triangles

When given the length of two sides and the measure of an angle that is not between the sides, a triangle can be drawn.

Draw a triangle that has sides of 2 inches and $1\frac{1}{2}$ inches and a non-included angle of 45°.

Step 1: Draw a line of any length.

Step 2: Use a protractor to draw a 2-inch line that creates the desired angle with the first line (45°).

Step 3: Use a compass set at $1\frac{1}{2}$ inches to find where the third line will intersect the base.

Step 4: Label the triangle.

2 in. $1\frac{1}{2}$ in.

45°

Use the angles and side lengths given to create triangles. Label the measurements on your drawing.

	a	**b**
1.	angle: 50° sides: 1 inch and 2 inches	angle: 140° sides: 3 cm and 4 cm
2.	angle: 85° sides: 2 inches and 4 inches	angle: 100° sides: 2 cm and 5 cm

Lesson 5.3 Drawing Geometric Shapes: Triangles

When given the lengths of three line segments, determine if the segments make a triangle by examining their relationship. Each pair of sides added together must be greater than the remaining side.

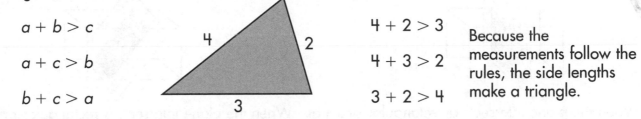

$a + b > c$

$a + c > b$

$b + c > a$

$4 + 2 > 3$

$4 + 3 > 2$

$3 + 2 > 4$

Because the measurements follow the rules, the side lengths make a triangle.

Using the given lengths, determine if they will make a triangle. Circle *yes* or *no*.

	a	**b**	**c**
1.	Side 1: 5 inches Side 2: 3 inches Side 3: 2 inches	Side 1: 3 feet Side 2: 8 feet Side 3: 7 feet	Side 1: 10 inches Side 2: 4 inches Side 3: 12 inches
	yes no	yes no	yes no
2.	Side 1: 5 centimeters Side 2: 8 centimeters Side 3: 20 centimeters	Side 1: 5 meters Side 2: 9 meters Side 3: 20 meters	Side 1: 10 inches Side 2: 10 inches Side 3: 19 inches
	yes no	yes no	yes no
3.	Side 1: 4 millimeters Side 2: 9 millimeters Side 3: 9 millimeters	Side 1: 4 inches Side 2: 4 inches Side 3: 7 inches	Side 1: 7 centimeters Side 2: 5 centimeters Side 3: 14 centimeters
	yes no	yes no	yes no
4.	Side 1: 3 centimeters Side 2: 3 centimeters Side 3: 10 centimeters	Side 1: 4 yards Side 2: 8 yards Side 3: 6 yards	Side 1: 2 meters Side 2: 3 meters Side 3: 4 meters
	yes no	yes no	yes no

Lesson 5.4 Cross Sections of 3-Dimensional Figures

A **cross section** of a 3-dimensional figure is the place where a plane cuts through the figure. The shape and size of the cross section depends on where the plane slices the figure.

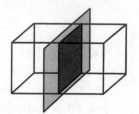

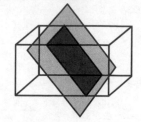

When the plane intersects a rectangular prism at a right angle, another rectangle is created.

When the plane intersects a rectangular prism at an angle, it will create a quadrilateral, but not necessarily a rectangle.

Name the shape that is created by the cross section.

a	b

1.

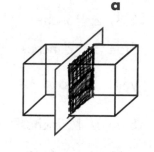

_____

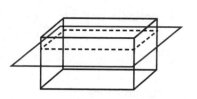

_____

2.

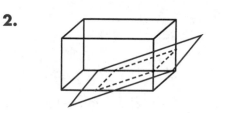

_____

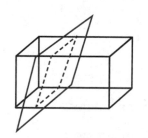

_____

3.

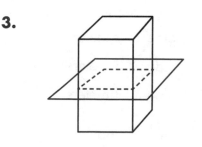

_____

_____

Lesson 5.4 Cross Sections of 3-Dimensional Figures

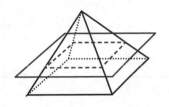

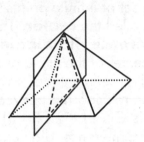

When the plane intersects a square pyramid parallel to the base, a square is created.

When the plane intersects a square pyramid at a 90° angle to the base, a triangle is created.

Tell what shape is created by the cross section.

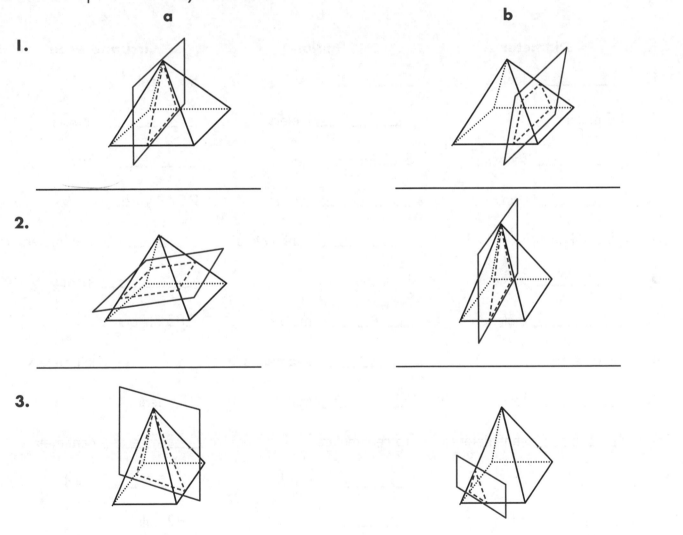

a

b

1.

_____

_____

2.

_____

_____

3.

_____

_____

Lesson 5.5 Circles: Circumference

A **circle** is a set of infinite points that are all the same distance from a given point, called the **center**. The perimeter of a circle is called the **circumference**. The **diameter** is a segment that passes through the center of the circle and has both endpoints on the circle. The **radius** is a segment that has as its endpoints the circle and the center. The relationship between the circumference (C) and the diameter (d) is $C \div d = \pi$. Pi (π) is approximately $3\frac{1}{7}$ or 3.14. To find the circumference, diameter, or radius of a circle, use the formulas $C = \pi \times d$ or $C = 2 \times \pi \times r$.

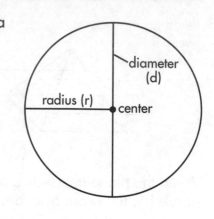

Complete the table. Use 3.14 for π.

	a Diameter	b Radius	c Circumference
1.	_____ feet	_____ feet	4.71 feet
2.	3.5 meters	_____ meters	_____ meters
3.	_____ inches	3.25 inches	_____ inches
4.	_____ yards	_____ yards	26.69 yards
5.	7.5 centimeters	_____ centimeters	_____ centimeters
6.	_____ inches	15 inches	_____ inches
7.	_____ meters	_____ meters	7.85 meters
8.	5 kilometers	_____ kilometers	_____ kilometers
9.	_____ feet	_____ feet	31.4 feet
10.	_____ centimeters	45 centimeters	_____ centimeters
11.	4 yards	_____ yards	_____ yards
12.	_____ miles	_____ miles	9.42 miles

Lesson 5.5 Circles: Circumference

Complete the chart for each circle described below. Use 3.14 for π. When necessary, round to the nearest hundredth.

	a Radius	b Diameter	c Circumference
1.	2 m	_____ m	_____ m
2.	_____ cm	18 cm	_____ cm
3.	_____ mm	9.2 mm	_____ mm
4.	5.5 in.	_____ in.	_____ in.
5.	12.2 cm	_____ cm	_____ cm
6.	_____ ft.	5 ft.	_____ ft.
7.	17 mm	_____ mm	_____ mm
8.	$3\frac{1}{2}$ ft.	_____ ft.	_____ ft.
9.	_____ cm	13 cm	_____ cm
10.	_____ yd.	3.8 yd.	_____ yd.
11.	3 cm	_____ cm	_____ cm
12.	_____ m	7 m	_____ m
13.	_____ km	4 km	_____ km
14.	4.5 in.	_____ in.	_____ in.
15.	5.6 mm	_____ mm	_____ mm

Lesson 5.5 Circles: Circumference

Find the circumference for each circle below. Use 3.14 for π. When necessary, round to the nearest hundredth.

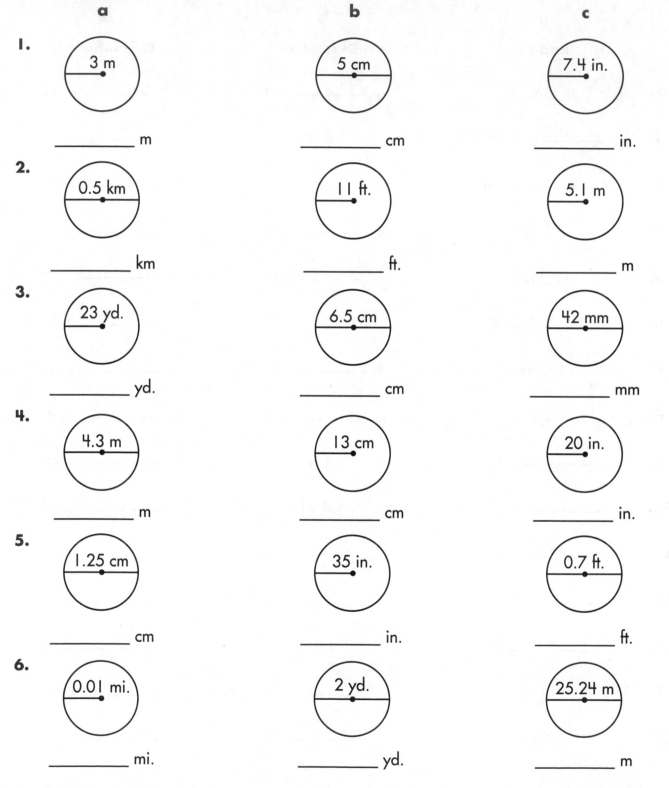

a	b	c
1. 3 m	5 cm	7.4 in.
_____ m	_____ cm	_____ in.
2. 0.5 km	11 ft.	5.1 m
_____ km	_____ ft.	_____ m
3. 23 yd.	6.5 cm	42 mm
_____ yd.	_____ cm	_____ mm
4. 4.3 m	13 cm	20 in.
_____ m	_____ cm	_____ in.
5. 1.25 cm	35 in.	0.7 ft.
_____ cm	_____ in.	_____ ft.
6. 0.01 mi.	2 yd.	25.24 m
_____ mi.	_____ yd.	_____ m

Lesson 5.6 Circles: Area

To find the area of a circle, use the formula A = π × r². Remember, the radius (r) is half the diameter. It is the distance from the center of the circle to its outer edge.

Find the area of each circle below. Use 3.14 for π. Round your answer to the nearest tenth.

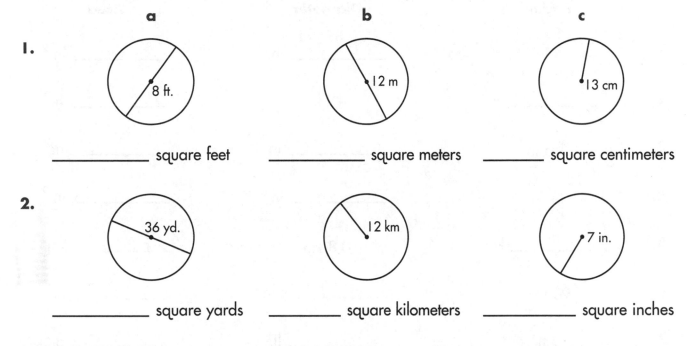

a	b	c

1.

_____ square feet   _____ square meters   _____ square centimeters

2.

_____ square yards   _____ square kilometers   _____ square inches

Complete the chart for each circle described below. Use 3.14 for π. When necessary, round to the nearest tenth.

	Diameter	Radius	Area
3.	_____ inches	3 inches	_____ square inches
4.	18 feet	_____ feet	_____ square feet
5.	17 meters	_____ meters	_____ square meters
6.	_____ centimeters	32 centimeters	_____ square centimeters

Lesson 5.6 Circles: Area

Complete the chart for each circle described below. Use 3.14 for π. When necessary, round to the nearest hundredth.

	a **Radius**	**b** **Diameter**	**c** **Area**
1.	4 in.	_____ in.	_____ in.²
2.	_____ ft.	12 ft.	_____ ft.²
3.	1.5 m	_____ m	_____ m²
4.	11 in.	_____ in.	_____ in.²
5.	_____ km	0.8 km	_____ km²
6.	90 mm	_____ mm	_____ mm²
7.	5 ft.	_____ ft.	_____ ft.²
8.	_____ in.	9 in.	_____ in.²
9.	_____ cm	8.2 cm	_____ cm²
10.	_____ m	11 m	_____ m²
11.	3 cm	_____ cm	_____ cm²
12.	12 in.	_____ in.	_____ in.²
13.	_____ km	28 km	_____ km²
14.	9 m	_____ m	_____ m²
15.	_____ cm	22 cm	_____ cm²

Lesson 5.6 Circles: Area

Find the area for each circle below. Use 3.14 for π. When necessary, round to the nearest hundredth.

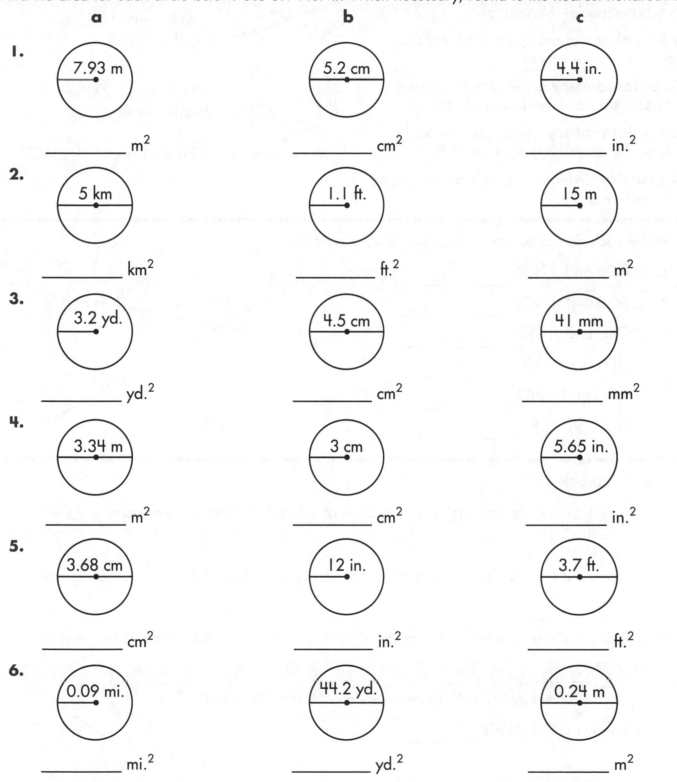

         a   **b**   **c**

1. 7.93 m   5.2 cm   4.4 in.

_____ m²   _____ cm²   _____ in.²

2. 5 km   1.1 ft.   15 m

_____ km²   _____ ft.²   _____ m²

3. 3.2 yd.   4.5 cm   41 mm

_____ yd.²   _____ cm²   _____ mm²

4. 3.34 m   3 cm   5.65 in.

_____ m²   _____ cm²   _____ in.²

5. 3.68 cm   12 in.   3.7 ft.

_____ cm²   _____ in.²   _____ ft.²

6. 0.09 mi.   44.2 yd.   0.24 m

_____ mi.²   _____ yd.²   _____ m²

Lesson 5.7 Angle Relationships

When two lines intersect, they form angles that have special relationships.

Vertical angles are opposite angles that have the same measure.

Supplementary angles are two angles whose measures have a sum of 180°.

Complementary angles are two angles whose measures have a sum of 90°.

A **bisector** divides an angle into two angles of equal measure.

∠ABC and ∠DBE are vertical.

∠ABD and ∠DBE are supplementary.

∠WXZ and ∠ZXY are complementary.

$\overrightarrow{XZ}$ is the bisector of ∠WXY.

Identify each pair of angles as *supplementary* or *vertical*.

1. ∠AGB and ∠HGE _____

2. ∠BGE and ∠HGE _____

3. ∠GEC and ∠CED _____

4. ∠GEC and ∠DEF _____

5. ∠AGH and ∠BGE _____

6. ∠GEF and ∠DEF _____

Solve each problem.

7. ∠A and ∠G are vertical angles. The measure of ∠A is 72°. What is the measure of ∠G?

   _____

8. ∠Y and ∠Z are supplementary angles. The measure of ∠Y is 112°. What is the measure of ∠Z? _____

9. ∠A and ∠B are complementary angles. The measure of ∠A is 53°. What is the measure of ∠B? _____

10. ∠RST is bisected by ray SW. The measure of ∠WST is 30°, what is the measure of ∠RST? _____

Lesson 5.7 Angle Relationships

Use the figure at the right to answer questions 1–6.

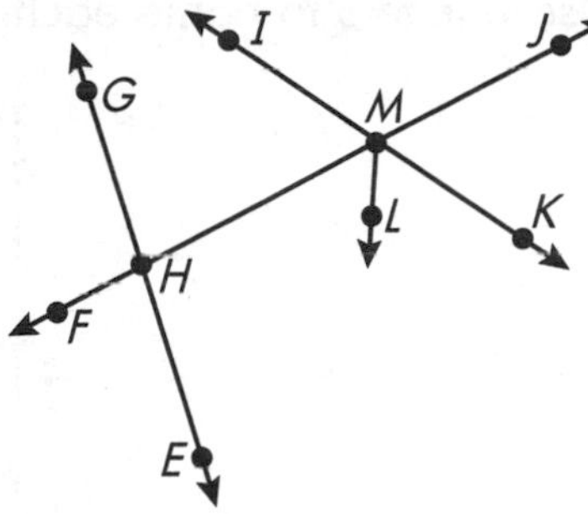

1. Name an angle that is vertical to ∠EHF. _____

2. Name an angle that is vertical to ∠EHM. _____

3. Name an angle that is supplementary to ∠IMJ. _____

4. Name the bisector of ∠HMK. _____

5. Name an angle that is vertical to ∠JMK. _____

6. Name an angle that is supplementary to ∠JMK. _____

Use the figure at the right to answer questions 7–10.

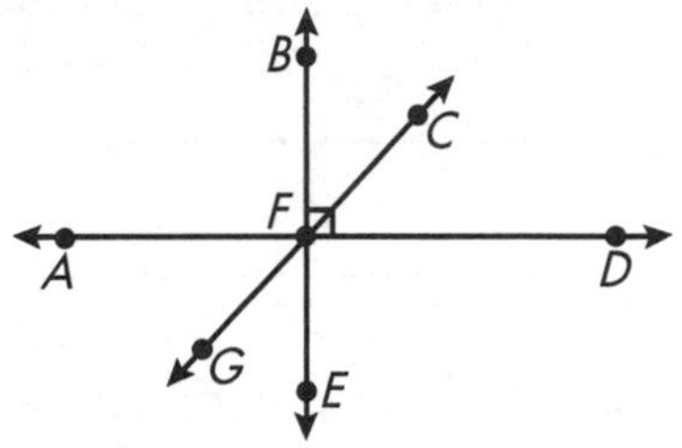

7. Name an angle complementary to ∠BFC. _____

8. Name an angle complementary to ∠AFG. _____

9. Name an angle that is supplementary to ∠CFD. _____

10. Name an angle that is supplementary to ∠GFE. _____

Solve.

11. ∠RST is supplementary to angle ∠PSO. The measure of ∠RST is 103°.

What is the measure of ∠PSO? _____

12. ∠MNO and ∠NOP are complementary. The measure of ∠NOP is 22°.

What is the measure of ∠MNO? _____

13. ∠XYZ is bisected by $\overrightarrow{YW}$. The measure of ∠XYW is 52°.

What is the measure of ∠WYZ? What is the measure of ∠XYZ?

The measure of ∠WYZ is _____.   The measure of ∠XYZ is _____.

14. ∠BCD is bisected by $\overrightarrow{CE}$. The measure of ∠DCE is 79°.

What is the measure of ∠BCE? What is the measure of ∠BCD?

The measure of ∠BCE is _____.   The measure of ∠BCD is _____.

Lesson 5.7 Angle Relationships

Use 3 letters to name each angle in the figures below.

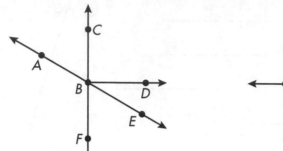 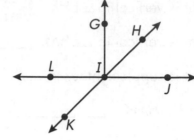

1. Which pairs of angles are complementary?

∠ _____ /∠ _____ , ∠ _____ /∠ _____

2. Which pairs of angles are supplementary?

∠ _____ /∠ _____ , ∠ _____ /∠ _____ , ∠ _____ /∠ _____ , ∠ _____ /∠ _____ , ∠ _____ /∠ _____

∠ _____ /∠ _____ , ∠ _____ /∠ _____ , ∠ _____ /∠ _____ , ∠ _____ /∠ _____ , ∠ _____ /∠ _____

3. Which pairs of angles are vertical angles?

∠ _____ /∠ _____ , ∠ _____ /∠ _____ , ∠ _____ /∠ _____ , ∠ _____ /∠ _____

4. Name a point on an angle bisector. _____

5. Which angle does the angle bisector named in question 4 bisect? _____

Mark the right angles on the figures above. Then, solve each problem.

6. If ∠DBE measures 39°, what does ∠FBE measure? _____

7. If ∠HIJ measures 45°, what does ∠KIJ measure? _____

8. If ∠LIH measures 135°, what does ∠KIJ measure? _____

9. If ∠CBE measures 131°, what does ∠DBE measure? _____

10. If ∠ABD measures 149°, what does ∠ABC measure? _____

Lesson 5.8 Problem Solving

SHOW YOUR WORK

Use angle relationships to solve the problems.

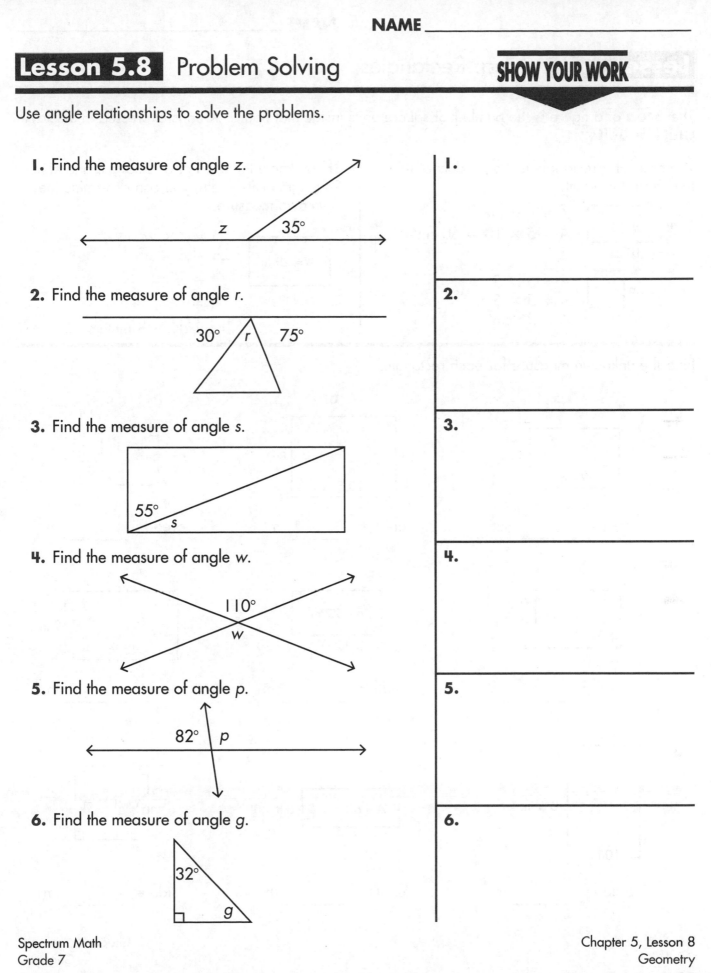

1. Find the measure of angle z.

z   35°

2. Find the measure of angle r.

30° r 75°

3. Find the measure of angle s.

55°
s

4. Find the measure of angle w.

110°
w

5. Find the measure of angle p.

82° p

6. Find the measure of angle g.

32°
g

1.

2.

3.

4.

5.

6.

Lesson 5.9 Area: Rectangles

The **area** of a figure is the number of square units inside that figure. Area is expressed in **square units** or **units^2**.

The area of a rectangle is the product of its length and its width.

5 cm ⬜ 10 cm

$A = \ell \times w$
$A = 5 \times 10 = 50 \text{ cm}^2$

5 cm ⬜

$A = 5 \times 5$
$A = 5 \times 5 \text{ or } 5^2$
$A = 25 \text{ cm}^2$

If you know the area of a rectangle and either its length or its width, you can determine the unknown measure.

$A = 24 \text{ m}^2$ 6 m

$A = \ell \times w$
$24 = 6 \times w$
$\frac{24}{6} = \frac{6w}{6}$
$4 = w$

The width is 4 meters.

Find the unknown measure for each rectangle.

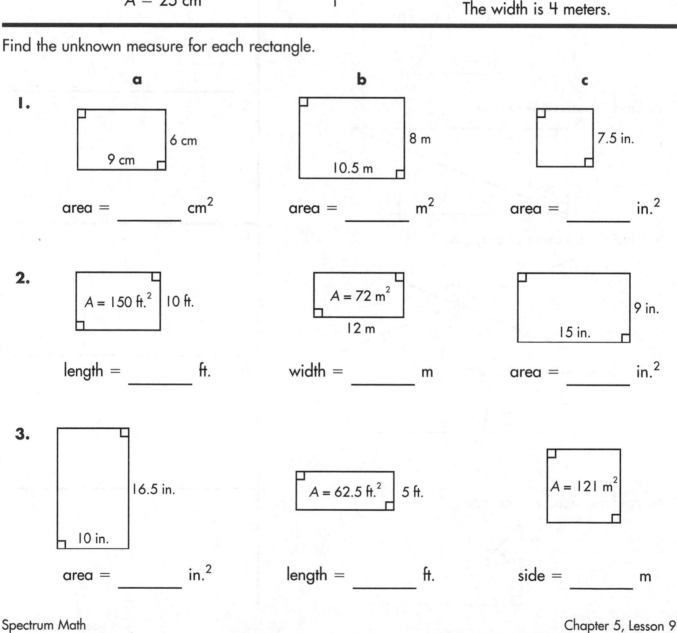

	a	**b**	**c**
1.	6 cm, 9 cm	8 m, 10.5 m	7.5 in.
	area = _____ cm^2	area = _____ m^2	area = _____ in.^{2}
2.	A = 150 ft.^{2}, 10 ft.	A = 72 m^2, 12 m	9 in., 15 in.
	length = _____ ft.	width = _____ m	area = _____ in.^{2}
3.	16.5 in., 10 in.	A = 62.5 ft.^{2}, 5 ft.	A = 121 m^2
	area = _____ in.^{2}	length = _____ ft.	side = _____ m

Lesson 5.10 Area: Triangles

To find the area of a triangle, find $\frac{1}{2}$ the product of the measure of its base and its height.

$$A = \frac{1}{2} \times b \times h$$

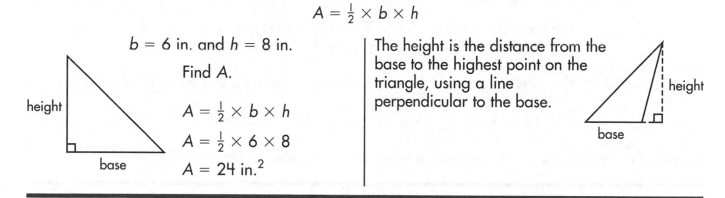

$b = 6$ in. and $h = 8$ in.

Find A.

$A = \frac{1}{2} \times b \times h$

$A = \frac{1}{2} \times 6 \times 8$

$A = 24$ in.^{2}

The height is the distance from the base to the highest point on the triangle, using a line perpendicular to the base.

Find the area of each triangle.

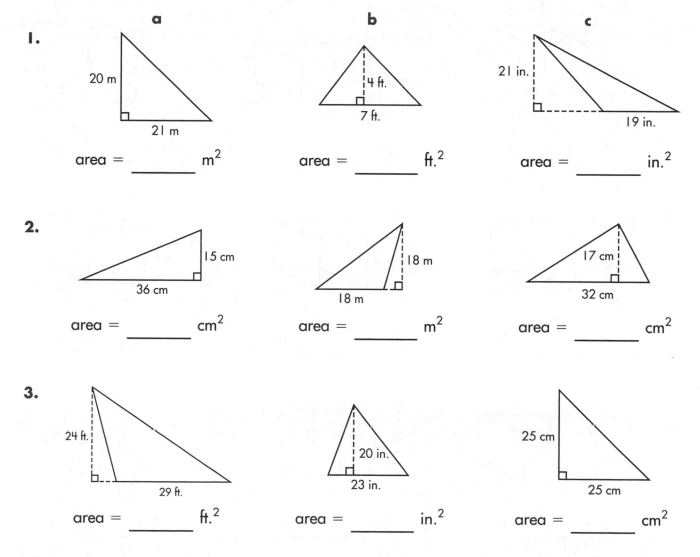

	a	b	c
1.	20 m, 21 m	4 ft., 7 ft.	21 in., 19 in.
	area = _____ m^2	area = _____ ft.^{2}	area = _____ in.^{2}
2.	15 cm, 36 cm	18 m, 18 m	17 cm, 32 cm
	area = _____ cm^2	area = _____ m^2	area = _____ cm^2
3.	24 ft., 29 ft.	20 in., 23 in.	25 cm, 25 cm
	area = _____ ft.^{2}	area = _____ in.^{2}	area = _____ cm^2

Lesson 5.11 Volume: Rectangular Prisms

Volume is the amount of space a solid (three-dimensional) figure occupies. You can calculate the volume of a rectangular solid by multiplying the area of its base by its height: $V = Bh$.

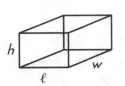

The area of the base is found by multiplying length and width. $B = \ell \times w$, so the volume can be found by using the formula $V = \ell \times w \times h$.

If $\ell = 10$ m, $w = 11$ m, and $h = 7$ m, what is the volume of the solid?

$V = 10 \times 11 \times 7$ $V = 770$ m^3 or 770 cubic meters.

Because the measure is in 3 dimensions, it is measured in **cubic units** or **units**^{3}.

Find the volume of each rectangular solid.

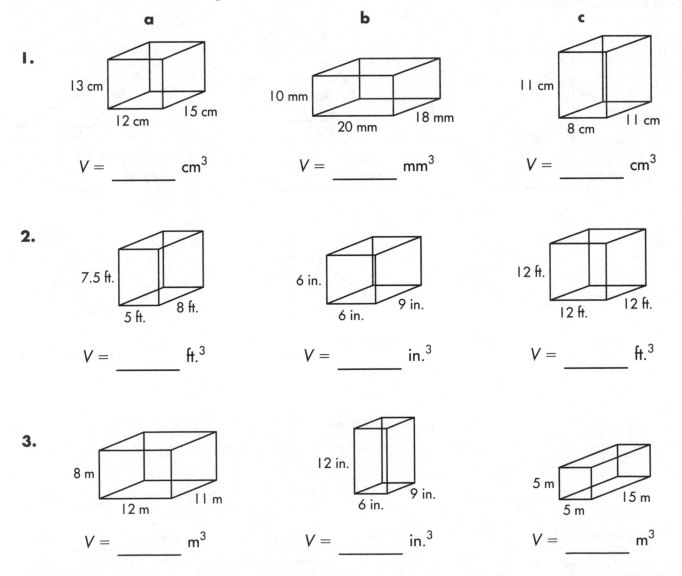

	a	b	c

1.

a: 13 cm, 12 cm, 15 cm $V = $ _____ cm^3

b: 10 mm, 20 mm, 18 mm $V = $ _____ mm^3

c: 11 cm, 8 cm, 11 cm $V = $ _____ cm^3

2.

a: 7.5 ft., 5 ft., 8 ft. $V = $ _____ ft.^{3}

b: 6 in., 6 in., 9 in. $V = $ _____ in.^{3}

c: 12 ft., 12 ft., 12 ft. $V = $ _____ ft.^{3}

3.

a: 8 m, 12 m, 11 m $V = $ _____ m^3

b: 12 in., 6 in., 9 in. $V = $ _____ in.^{3}

c: 5 m, 5 m, 15 m $V = $ _____ m^3

Lesson 5.12 Volume: Pyramids

Volume is the amount of space a solid figure occupies. The **volume of a pyramid** is calculated as $\frac{1}{3}$ base $\times$ height. This is because a pyramid occupies $\frac{1}{3}$ of the volume of a rectangular prism of the same height. Because the base of a square pyramid is square, $B = s^2$.

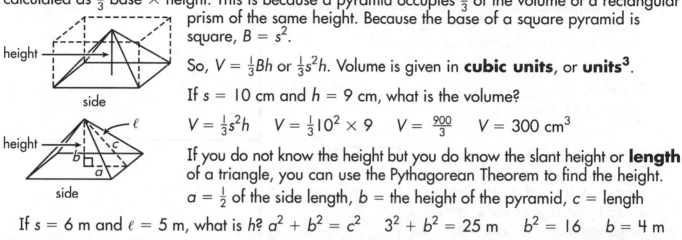

So, $V = \frac{1}{3}Bh$ or $\frac{1}{3}s^2h$. Volume is given in **cubic units**, or **units^3**.

If $s = 10$ cm and $h = 9$ cm, what is the volume?

$V = \frac{1}{3}s^2h \quad V = \frac{1}{3}10^2 \times 9 \quad V = \frac{900}{3} \quad V = 300 \text{ cm}^3$

If you do not know the height but you do know the slant height or **length** of a triangle, you can use the Pythagorean Theorem to find the height. $a = \frac{1}{2}$ of the side length, $b =$ the height of the pyramid, $c =$ length

If $s = 6$ m and $\ell = 5$ m, what is h? $a^2 + b^2 = c^2 \quad 3^2 + b^2 = 25 \text{ m} \quad b^2 = 16 \quad b = 4 \text{ m}$

Find the volume of each pyramid. Round answers to the nearest hundredth.

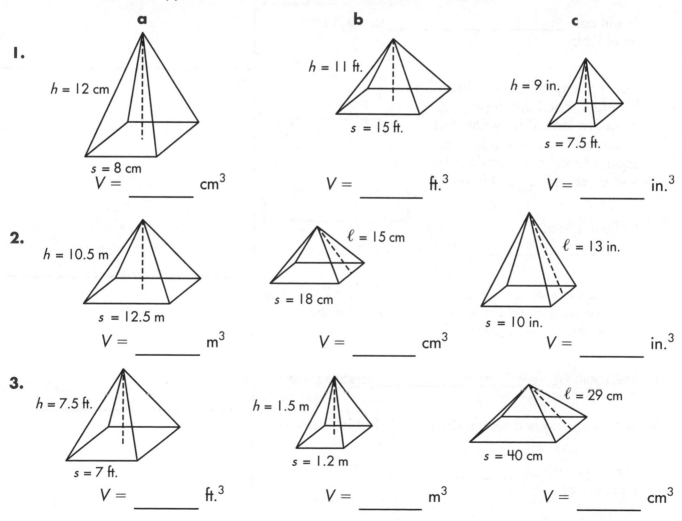

a

1. $h = 12$ cm, $s = 8$ cm
$V =$ _____ cm^3

2. $h = 10.5$ m, $s = 12.5$ m
$V =$ _____ m^3

3. $h = 7.5$ ft., $s = 7$ ft.
$V =$ _____ ft.^{3}

b

1. $h = 11$ ft., $s = 15$ ft.
$V =$ _____ ft.^{3}

2. $\ell = 15$ cm, $s = 18$ cm
$V =$ _____ cm^3

3. $h = 1.5$ m, $s = 1.2$ m
$V =$ _____ m^3

c

1. $h = 9$ in., $s = 7.5$ ft.
$V =$ _____ in.^{3}

2. $\ell = 13$ in., $s = 10$ in.
$V =$ _____ in.^{3}

3. $\ell = 29$ cm, $s = 40$ cm
$V =$ _____ cm^3

Lesson 5.13 Problem Solving

SHOW YOUR WORK

Solve each problem.

1. On a map, each centimeter represents 45 kilometers. Two towns are 135 kilometers apart. What is the distance between the towns on the map?

   The towns are _____ centimeters apart on the map.

   1.

2. This hotel lobby is being carpeted. Each unit length represents 1 yard. Carpet costs $22.50 per square yard. How much will it cost to carpet the room?

   It will cost _____ to carpet the hotel lobby.

   2.

3. Hal is going to put tiles down for his patio. Each unit represents 1 square foot. If he wants this shape and tiles cost $3.15 per square foot, how much will Hal end up spending for his patio?

   Hal will spend

   _____ to tile his patio.

   3.

4. A scale drawing shows a room as 10 cm by 7 cm. The scale of the drawing is 2 cm = 5 m. What is the actual area of the room?

   The room is _____ square meters.

   4.

5. A circular rug is 8 feet in diameter. What is its area?

   The rug's area is _____ square feet.

   5.

Lesson 5.13 Problem Solving

Solve each problem.

1. Shawn built a fort in his yard that is 6 feet tall and 6 feet long on all sides. He wants to paint the inside of it (walls, ceiling, and floor). If each bucket of paint will cover 300 square feet, how many buckets of paint should Shawn buy?

   Shawn will need to buy _____ bucket of paint.

2. Find the surface area of this figure.

   The surface area is _____ square meters.

3. Rita builds a pool in her backyard. The pool measures 60 feet long, 32 feet wide, and 8 feet deep. How much water will fit in the pool?

   _____ cubic feet of water will fit in the pool.

4. Carrie bought a gift that is inside a box that is 3 feet by 2 feet by 3 feet. How much wrapping paper is needed to cover the box?

   Carrie needs _____ square feet of wrapping paper.

5. The rectangular top of a table is twice as long as it is wide. Its width is $1\frac{1}{4}$ meters. What is the area of the tabletop?

   The tabletop is _____ square meters.

6. Ian bought enough carpet to cover 500 square feet. He wants to cover a room that is 10 feet 5 inches long by 9 feet 7 inches. About how much will he have left over for the rest of the house?

   Ian will have about _____ square feet left over.

1.

2.

3.

4.

5.

6.

Lesson 5.13 Problem Solving

Solve each problem.

1. A cereal box is shaped like a rectangular prism with a height of 14 in., length of 8 in., and width of 3 in. How much cereal will fit in the box?

   _____ cubic inches of cereal will fit in the box?

2. Mr. and Mrs. Hastings are adding a basement to their house. The basement will be 40 feet by 25 feet by 10 feet. How much dirt will have to be removed from under the house to make room for the construction?

   _____ cubic feet of dirt will have to be removed.

3. Jonas is going to have a square cake for his birthday. The cake will be made with two layers that measure 12 inches by 12 inches by $1\frac{1}{2}$ inches. How much icing will be needed to cover the cake, including putting icing between the layers?

   Jonas will need _____ square inches of icing.

4. The glass for a picture frame that is 10 inches by 12 inches has broken. A new piece of glass costs $0.35 per square inch. How much will a new piece of glass cost?

   The glass will cost _____.

5. An Olympic-size swimming pool measures 50 meters by 15 meters. What size pool cover will be needed to cover the pool for the winter?

   A pool cover that is _____ square meters will be needed.

6. Ebony built a model of an Egyptian pyramid. Her model measures 0.5 meters along the bottom of one side and 0.3 meters tall. What is the volume of her pyramid?

   Ebony's pyramid has a volume of _____ cubic meters.

1.

2.

3.

4.

5.

6.

Check What You Learned

Geometry

Find the area of each figure.

a   **b**   **c**

1.

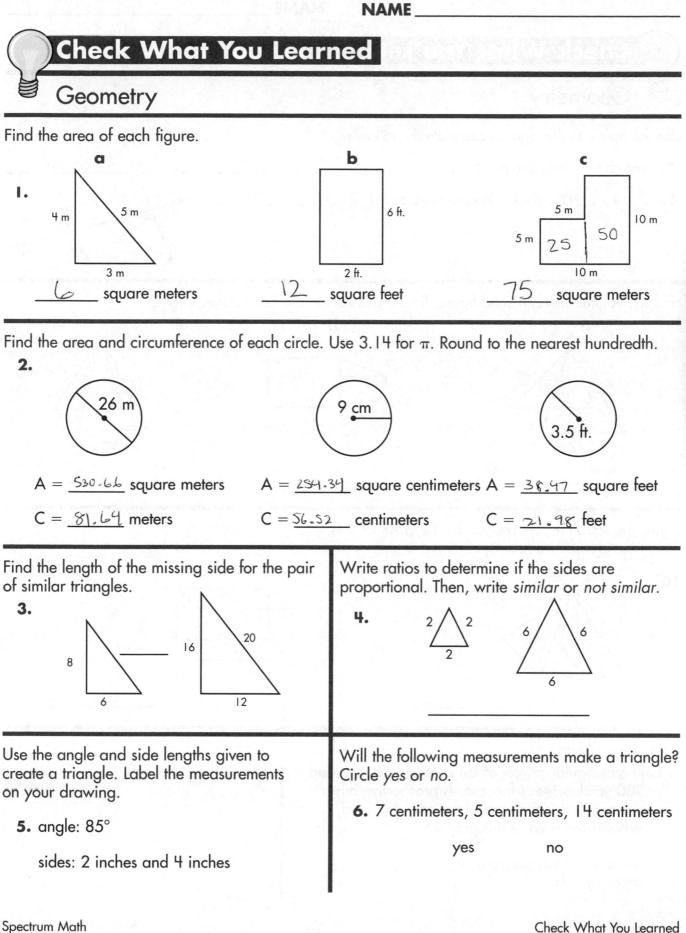

4 m   5 m

3 m

___6___ square meters

6 ft.

2 ft.

___12___ square feet

5 m
5 m   25   50   10 m
10 m

___75___ square meters

Find the area and circumference of each circle. Use 3.14 for π. Round to the nearest hundredth.

2.

26 m   9 cm   3.5 ft.

A = __530.66__ square meters   A = __254.34__ square centimeters A = __38.47__ square feet

C = __81.64__ meters   C = __56.52__ centimeters   C = __21.98__ feet

Find the length of the missing side for the pair of similar triangles.

3.

8   16   20

6   12

Write ratios to determine if the sides are proportional. Then, write *similar* or *not similar*.

4.

2 2   6 6
  2   6

_____

Use the angle and side lengths given to create a triangle. Label the measurements on your drawing.

5. angle: 85°

sides: 2 inches and 4 inches

Will the following measurements make a triangle? Circle *yes* or *no*.

6. 7 centimeters, 5 centimeters, 14 centimeters

yes   no

CHAPTER 5 POSTTEST

Check What You Learned

Geometry

Use the figure to the right to complete the following.

7. Which two lines are parallel? _____

8. If ∠11 is 70°, what is the measure of ∠10? _____

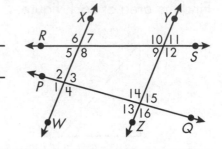

Find the volume of each solid figure. Round answers to the nearest hundredth.

a   **b**   **c**

9.

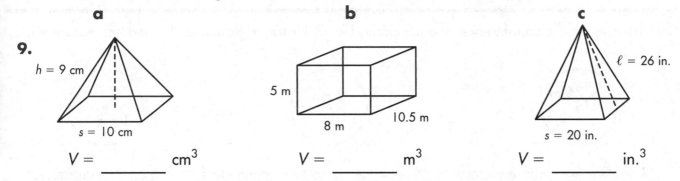

a: $h = 9$ cm, $s = 10$ cm

$V =$ _____ cm^3

b: 5 m, 8 m, 10.5 m

$V =$ _____ m^3

c: $\ell = 26$ in., $s = 20$ in.

$V =$ _____ in.^{3}

Name the shape that is created by the cross section.

a   **b**

10.

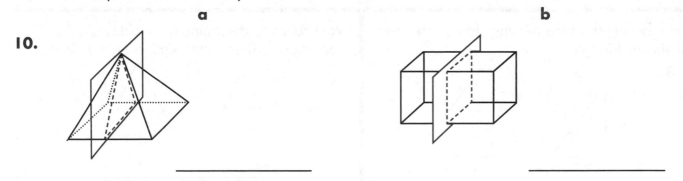

_____   _____

Solve the problem.

11. A rectangular parcel of land 121 yards long and 200 yards wide is for sale. A prospective buyer wants to know the area of the parcel of land. What is the area of this property?

The area of this property is _____ square yards.

11.

Check What You Know

Statistics

Tell if each is an example of a *sample* or a *population*.

a	b

1. 10 students' heights are measured   every student's time of arrival at school is recorded

_____   _____

2. every 5th water bottle is checked   a teacher records all students' test grades

_____   _____

Tell if each sample would be considered *random* or *biased*.

3. Felicia wants to know what middle school students' favorite sports are. She asks 20 people leaving a football game. _____

4. Mr. Walsh puts every 7th grader's name into a jar. He shakes the jar and pulls out 4 students' names. _____

Complete the following items based on the data set below.

Joe records the daily high temperature every other day for one month. This is the information he collects about the daily high temperature in Fahrenheit:

66, 68, 72, 79, 67, 82, 73, 85, 68, 81, 73, 82, 69, 73, 74

5. Create a stem-and-leaf plot for the data.

6. Find the mean, median, mode, and range of the data.

mean: _____   mode: _____

median: _____   range: _____

NAME _____

Check What You Know

Statistics

Continue using the data set below to answer the questions.

Joe records the daily high temperature every other day for one month. This is the information he collects about the daily high temperature in Fahrenheit:

66, 68, 72, 79, 67, 82, 73, 85, 68, 81, 73, 82, 69, 73, 74

7. How many days from the sample were above 70 degrees? _____

8. What percentage of days from the sample were 69 degrees or less? _____

9. Based on a 30-day month, how many days were most likely above 80 degrees? _____

Use the two data sets below to answer the questions.

Juanita gathered information about the sizes of oranges and grapefruits. She chose 10 of each from the grocery store to weigh.

Weight of oranges (oz.)	Weight of grapefruits (oz.)
7.0, 7.5, 7.2, 6.5, 7.8, 7.3, 7.4, 7.7, 7.5, 7.2	10.2, 8.9, 9.4, 9.5, 10.0, 8.9, 9.2, 9.6, 10.1, 9.6
a	**b**

10. Draw a histogram for each set of data.

11. Find the measures of center and range for each set of data.

mean: _____   mean: _____

median: _____   median: _____

mode: _____   mode: _____

range: _____   range: _____

12. Tell one way the data sets are alike and one way they are different.

alike: _____   different: _____

Lesson 6.1 Sampling

When a **population**, or data set, has a very large number of data points, sampling can be used to help summarize the data set.

To be sure that the description of the population is correct, **random sampling** should be used. If a summary is made based on **biased sampling**, the description of the population will not be accurate.

Diana is trying to find out what kind of music 7th graders prefer. If she was to interview the first 60 seventh graders to arrive at school one morning, she would be using random sampling because school arrival time has nothing to do with taste in music. If she was to interview 60 7th graders who are taking band, or who are at a concert for a specific band, she would be using biased sampling because both of those factors can affect someone's taste in music.

Tell if each sample would be considered *random* or *biased*.

1. Charlie puts a deck of cards in a bag. He shakes the bag and pulls 4 cards out of the bag.

   _____ r _____

2. Nicole wanted to know what 6th graders' favorite movie of the year was. She asked 10 girls from her homeroom class.

   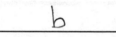
   _____ b _____

3. A garden has 100 pepper plants. John wants to know the number of peppers that are on each of the plants. He counts the number of peppers on the plants in one of the outside rows.

   _____ b _____

4. Ben wants to know what time most 7th graders get on the bus in the morning. He surveys five students from each bus.

   _____ r _____

5. Anna wants to know how much middle school students weigh. She weighs 1 student from each homeroom.

   _____ r _____

6. Jordan wants to know which restaurant makes the best burger in town. He stands on a block between two different burger restaurants at dinner time and asks the first 25 people that walk by.

   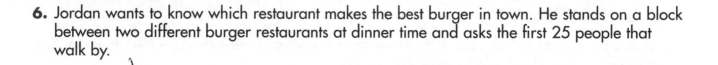
   _____ b _____

Lesson 6.1 Sampling

When sampling a data set, there are several approaches that can be used to create a random sample.

Types of Random Samples	
Simple Random Sample	A sample is chosen that is as random as any other sample that could have been chosen.
Stratified Random Sample	The data set is divided into similar groups that do not overlap. Then, a sample is chosen from each group.
Systematic Random Sample	The sample is chosen starting from a specific point and continuing for a chosen interval.

There are also different ways of creating a biased sample.

Types of Biased Samples	
Convenience Sample	The sample is made up of data points that are easy to access instead of making an effort to gather a larger, more diverse sample.
Voluntary Response Sample	The data set is made up information from people who volunteered to participate. Volunteers are often biased toward one outcome.

Name the type of sampling used in each situation.

1. At a factory, every 100th piece is taken off the assembly line to be inspected.

   Sy - r

2. A reporter for the school newspaper asks 10 students in the cafeteria who would make the best student council president.

   S - r

3. Your math teacher calls on every 3rd name alphabetically to answer questions.

   Sy - r

4. 15 students from your school get to represent your school at a news conference. Everybody's names are put in a box by grade level and 5 names are drawn from each box.

   St - r

5. Shana announces to her class that she wants to know which new movie is their favorite. She calls on the first 10 people to raise their hands.

   V - re

Lesson 6.2 Drawing Inferences from Data

Data sets from random samples can be used to make inferences about the data from the population.

Billy is collecting information on how long his classmates spend studying each week. He talks to 11 different students from his class of 29 and collects the information show on the histogram below.

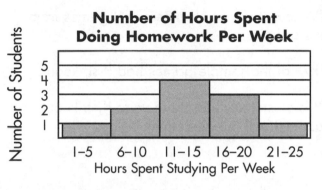

Number of Hours Spent Doing Homework Per Week

Number of Students

Hours Spent Studying Per Week

The following information can be determined using this data:

- 4 students spend 11–15 hours each week studying.
- 4 out of 11 is 36.36% of the sample.
- 36.36% of 29 is 10.54.
- This means that it is most likely that 10 or 11 students in Billy's class spend 11–15 hours each week studying.

Use the data below to make inferences and answer the questions.

This histogram shows the test scores from a sample of 30 students. There are 125 students in the 7th grade.

1. How many students from the sample scored between 70 and 80 on the test? 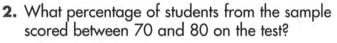 5

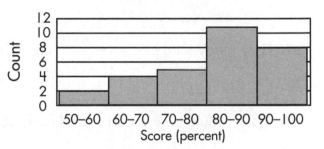

Test Scores of Students

Count

Score (percent)

2. What percentage of students from the sample scored between 70 and 80 on the test?

   16.67%

3. Predict how many students in the 7th grade scored between 70 and 80 on the test.

   20 or 21

4. What percentage of students from the sample scored between 90 and 100 on the test?

   26.67%

5. Based on the percentage of students from the sample who scored between 90 and 100 on the test, how many students in 7th grade scored between 90 and 100?

   33 or 34

6. If there were 150 students in 7th grade, how many students would have scored between 60 and 70 on the test?

   20

Lesson 6.2 Drawing Inferences from Data

The coach of the Wilson High School baseball team is collecting information about how well his pitchers are performing. He keeps data about every third game.

	Walks	Hits	Strikeouts
Game 3	2	1	4
Game 6	1	2	3
Game 9	0	1	4
Game 12	0	4	6
Game 15	3	5	1
Game 18	3	4	2
Game 21	2	6	4
Game 24	4	5	6
Game 27	2	4	4
Game 30	1	4	2

The following information can be inferred using this data:

• Pitchers struck out 4 hitters in 4 games from the sample.

• 40% of the sample games had 4 strikeouts.

• It is most likely that there were 4 strikeouts in about 12 of the 30 games.

Use the data above to answer the questions.

1. What percentage of the sample games had no walks?

_____

2. How many total hits were given up in the sample?

_____

3. What would be a realistic prediction about the number of total hits in 30 games?

_____

4. How many out of the 30 games were most likely to have had 5 or more hits?

_____

5. What percentage of the sample games had 2 walks?

_____

6. What would be a realistic prediction about the number of total games that had 2 walks?

_____

Lesson 6.2 Drawing Inferences from Data

Dawn is trying to find out how many brothers and sisters teachers in her school have. There are 54 teachers at the school, and she talks to 18 teachers. This is the data she collects: 1, 1, 1, 2, 0, 1, 2, 0, 1, 2, 4, 0, 1, 2, 3, 4, 5, 9.

This is the information that can be inferred about the data Dawn collected:

- 2 out of the 18 teachers sampled have 4 siblings.
- 11.11% of the teachers sampled have 4 siblings.
- It is most likely that 5 or 6 teachers at the school have 4 siblings.

Use the data below to answer the questions.

Mrs. Jones is giving a science test and she is trying to make sure students are spending enough time studying for the test. She chooses 5 students from each of her four classes and asks how many hours they spent studying. She collects the following information: $\frac{1}{2}$, $1\frac{1}{2}$, 3, 1, 2, $3\frac{1}{2}$, 1, $1\frac{1}{2}$, $1\frac{1}{2}$, 2, 3 $\frac{1}{2}$, 2, $1\frac{1}{2}$, 2, 2, $3\frac{1}{2}$, $2\frac{1}{2}$, $1\frac{1}{2}$, $3\frac{1}{2}$, 3.

1. How many students were included in Mrs. Jones's sample?

_____

2. If she has 25 students in each class, how many students are in her population?

_____

3. What percentage of the sample spent 2 hours studying for the test?

_____

4. Based on this sample, about how many students from all of the classes spent 2 hours studying for the test?

_____

5. Based on this sample, about how many students from all of the classes spent at least $2\frac{1}{2}$ hours studying for the test?

_____

6. Based on this sample, about how many students from all of the classes spent less than 2 hours studying for the test?

_____

Lesson 6.3 Reviewing Measures of Center

The **mean** is the average of a set of numbers. It is found by adding the set of numbers and then dividing by the number of addends.

The **median** is the middle number of a set of numbers that is ordered from least to greatest. When there is an even amount of numbers, it is the mean of the two middle numbers.

The **mode** is the number that appears most often in a set of numbers. There is no mode if all numbers appear the same number of times.

The **range** is the difference between the greatest and least numbers in the set.

Find the mean, median, mode, and range of the following set of numbers.

34, 32, 39, 33, 37, 36, 39, 38

mean: $34 + 32 + 39 + 33 + 37 + 36 + 39 + 38 = \frac{288}{8} = 36$

Arrange the numbers from least to greatest to find median, mode, and range.

32, 33, 34, 36, 37, 38, 39, 39

median: $\frac{36+37}{2} = 36.5$ mode: 39   range: $39 - 32 = 7$

Find the mean, median, mode, and range of the following sets of numbers.

	a	b
1.	8, 6, 9, 11, 12, 4, 9, 10, 9, 2	40.7, 23.1, 18.5, 43.6, 52.1, 50.9, 44.8, 23.1

  mean: _____   mean: _____

  median: _____   median: _____

  mode: _____   mode: _____

  range: _____   range: _____

2. 152, 136, 171, 208, 193, 163,   349, 562.5, 612, 349, 187, 612, 530,
   124, 212, 216, 171   716.5, 349, 902

  mean: _____   mean: _____

  median: _____   median: _____

  mode: _____   mode: _____

  range: _____   range: _____

Lesson 6.4 Comparing Similar Data Sets

Two data sets with similar characteristics can be compared by examining their distribution and measures of center.

Basketball Players' Heights (in.)	Football Players' Heights (in.)
69, 70, 72, 73, 73, 73, 74, 75, 75, 76	65, 66, 68, 69, 69, 70, 70, 71, 72

Compare the two data sets by setting them up on a graph.

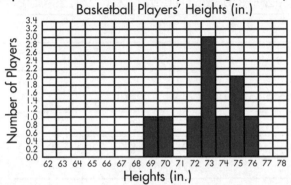

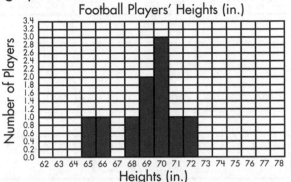

These data sets have a similar range, 7 for both. However, when we look at the data sets spread out along the same scale of measurement, we can see that basketball players are generally taller than football players. This can be verified by finding the mean height of basketball players (73 in.) and the mean height of football players (69 in.).

Examine the distributions and measures of center of the data sets below. Then, write 2 to 3 sentences that compare the sets.

1. Compare the calorie counts of 10 different menu items at popular fast food restaurants.

Restaurant 1	Restaurant 2
550, 520, 610, 600, 540, 750, 250, 670, 510, 590	320, 410, 360, 410, 380, 370, 290, 310, 320, 230

_____

_____

2. Compare the scores of two different science classes on the same science test.

Class 1	Class 2
78, 78, 78, 80, 85, 88, 90, 92, 100	85, 85, 90, 90, 92, 93, 95, 97, 97, 100

_____

_____

3. Compare the prices of 10 different items at a clothing store.

Store 1	Store 2
$10, $43, $6, $15, $20, $48, $68, $99, $47, $28	$12, $46, $8, $17, $19, $45, $68, $100, $48, $30

_____

_____

Lesson 6.4 Comparing Similar Data Sets

Examine the distributions and measures of center of the data sets below. Then, write 2 to 3 sentences that compare the sets.

I. Compare the word counts of 10 different pages from novels read in 5th grade and 8th grade.

5th Grade Word Count	8th Grade Word Count
255, 225, 260, 187, 260, 253, 252, 270, 255, 232	273, 275, 310, 255, 180, 265, 271, 273, 280, 305

_____

_____

2. Compare the amounts of money two families donate to charity over 1 year.

Family 1	Family 2
$25, $50, $25, $75, $25, $50, $75, $100, $50, $25, $25, $200	$50, $100, $75, $100, $500, $75, $200, $50, $50, $50, $75, $200

_____

_____

3. Compare family sizes in New York City and the United States.

Family Size in New York City	Family Size in United States
1, 2, 3, 1, 1, 3, 2, 1, 4, 2	2, 3, 1, 5, 4, 3, 4, 2, 6, 4

_____

_____

4. Compare the number of books read over the summer in two different 7th grade homeroom classes.

Homeroom A	Homeroom B
5, 9, 10, 15, 4, 3, 0, 9, 6, 7, 1, 2, 5, 10	6, 5, 7, 4, 8, 9, 9, 5, 10, 12, 15, 3, 0, 6

_____

_____

5. Compare the amounts of eggs each farm collected over 1 year.

Farm 1	Farm 2
21, 25, 24, 30, 20, 15, 18, 26, 15, 14, 17, 21	22, 23, 24, 22, 26, 21, 20, 19, 15, 20, 14, 21

_____

_____

Lesson 6.5 Problem Solving with Data

When a scientific question is identified, data can be collected based on an experiment. Then, the data can be compared using statistics.

Maria wants to know how much time she should spend studying for a test. She asks 15 classmates how long they studied for their last tests and then asks them how they scored on their tests. Here is the information she gathered:

Studied 0–2 Hours	80, 82, 90, 94, 85, 78, 82, 84
Studied More than 2 Hours	92, 94, 96, 88, 85, 90, 98

Studied 0–2 Hours

Stem	Leaf
7	8
8	0 2 2 4 5
9	0 4

Studied More than 2 Hours

Stem	Leaf
8	5 8
9	0 2 4 6 8

The mean score for the students who studied 0–2 hours is 84.38, and the mean for the students who studied 2 or more hours is 91.86. So, students who studied 2 or more hours had better results overall than students who studied 0–2 hours. For Maria to have the best possible result on her next test, she should study for 2 or more hours.

Analyze the data sets below to make an inference about the situation.

1. Robert wants to know how many hours of light are best for growing tomato plants. He plants 20 tomato plants that are all close together in height. He gives one group of 10 plants 4 hours of light every day and gives the other 10 plants 10 hours of light every day. He measures them at the end of 3 weeks to find out how much each plant has grown.

Growth for 4-hour plants (in.)	3, 5, 5, 6, 4, 6, 3, 4, 6, 4
Growth for 10-hour plants (in.)	9, 10, 12, 8, 10, 11, 9, 8, 8, 9

_____

_____

2. Cheri wants to find out how different activities affect tablet battery life. She tested 10 of the same tablet with full batteries. She had one group watch videos until the battery ran out. She had the other group play a game until the battery ran out. She measured how long it took each tablet battery to run out.

Battery life with videos (hr.)	5.4, 5.6, 6.0, 5.9, 5.6
Battery life with game (hr.)	7.6, 7.7, 7.7, 7.3, 7.4

_____

_____

Lesson 6.5 Problem Solving with Data

Analyze the data sets below to make an inference about the situation.

1. Samantha is on the track team and wonders if height plays a role in long-jump ability. She talked to 20 people at her last track meet to check their heights and see how far they jumped during the meet. Here is the data she collected:

Students who are 70 inches or taller (in.)	180, 161, 129, 115, 193, 154, 130, 109, 152, 160
Students who are less than 70 inches tall (in.)	165, 109, 129, 115, 150, 142, 136, 113, 121, 120

Inference:

_____

_____

2. Ms. Daniels is a math teacher and wonders if the amount of study time each night is related to how well students perform on final tests. She talked to 30 students in her math class to check their study times and compared that to their grades on the final math test. Here is the data she collected:

Less than an hour each night of study time	65, 75, 69, 81, 95, 62, 78, 84, 83, 55, 68, 75, 90, 68, 95
1 to 3 hours each night of study time	85, 95, 94, 89, 91, 75, 65, 93, 92, 90, 84, 89, 78, 90, 92

Inference:

_____

_____

3. Ross is a fisherman and wonders if how many pounds of bait you bring on a fishing trip is related to how many fish you catch. He talked to 20 fishermen at his marina to record the amount of bait brought and the amount of fish caught. Here is the data he collected:

50 pounds or less bait	18, 20, 15, 15, 14, 20, 25, 17, 19, 10
51 pounds or more bait	17, 18, 22, 22, 14, 13, 16, 19, 15, 11

Inference:

_____

_____

Check What You Learned

Statistics

Use the following data set to complete the problems.

Cars Across the Bridge Per Day	93, 105, 92, 111, 98, 97, 108, 101, 112, 115, 96, 104, 103, 91, 97

1. Make a stem-and-leaf plot to represent the data.

2. Find the mean, median, mode, and range of the data.

mean: _____   mode: _____

median: _____   range: _____

3. How many days did over 100 cars cross the bridge? _____

4. If the sample represents a 75-day time period, what is the most likely number of days that

over 100 cars crossed the bridge in that time? _____

5. How many days did between 90 and 95 cars cross the bridge? _____

6. What percentage of the sample represents between 90 and 95 cars crossing the bridge?

_____

Tell if each sample would be considered *random* or *biased*.

7. Lonnie wants to know where most people like to go on vacation.

He surveyed 20 people at a mountain town in Colorado. _____

8. Antonio wants to know what is the most popular type of book to read.

He surveyed 100 people coming out of a bookstore over a 3-day weekend. _____

NAME _____

Check What You Learned

Statistics

Use the data sets below to answer the questions.

Seven dogs and seven rabbits run around a track. Their times are listed below.

Dogs' Times (seconds)	Rabbits' Times (seconds)
6.3, 7.2, 6.5, 7.5, 7.1, 6.6, 6.4	5.4, 6.0, 5.6, 6.2, 4.9, 5.6, 6.2

                    a   **b**

9. Draw histograms to represent both sets of data.

10. Find the measures of center and range for both sets of data.

mean: _____   mean: _____

median: _____   median: _____

mode: _____   mode: _____

range: _____   range: _____

11. How are the two data sets alike and different?

alike: _____   different: _____

12. Based on this data, what is the difference between these two animals?

_____

Tell if each is an example of a *sample* or a *population*.

                    a   **b**

13. every 7ᵗʰ person's bag is checked at the airport   all children under the age of 2

_____   _____

Check What You Know

Probability

Complete a frequency table using the following data.

1. Daily High Temperature (°F): 66, 68, 72, 79, 67, 82, 73, 85, 68, 81, 73, 82, 69, 73, 74

Temperature	Frequency	Cumulative Frequency	Relative Frequency
66°–70°			%
71°–75°			%
76°–80°			%
81°–85°			%

Use the spinner to determine the probability of the following events. Write your answer as a fraction in simplest form.

2. spinning a gray section _____

3. spinning a 3 _____

4. spinning an even number _____

5. spinning a 2 _____

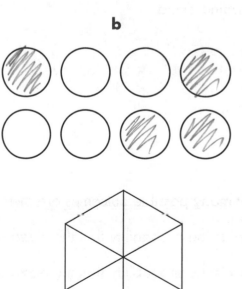

Color or label the shapes below so that the event will have uniform probability.

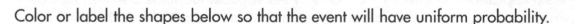

a   b

6.

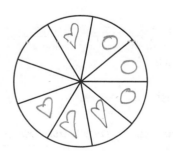

7.

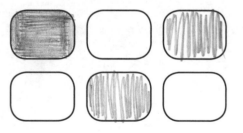

NAME _____

Check What You Know

Probability

Solve the problems below.

8. A bag is full of marbles. There are 27 green marbles, 33 red marbles, and 12 blue marbles.

   a. What is the probability of pulling out a red marble? _____

   b. What color is least likely to be pulled out of the bag? _____

9. A spinner is split into 8 sections. Five sections are red, 2 sections are blue, and 1 section has a star on it.

   a. What is the probability of landing on a blue section? _____

   b. What is the probability of landing on a red section? _____

10. Monica's closet has 9 shirts, 5 pairs of pants, and 4 pairs of shoes. How many combinations of outfits can she make that contain all 3 pieces of clothing?

   Monica can make _____ combinations of clothing.

Create a tree diagram and then answer the questions.

11. Pepi's Pizza has a choice of thin crust or thick crust. The available toppings are mushrooms, onions, pepperoni, and sausage. Make a tree diagram showing the possible outcomes for a 1-topping pizza.

12. How many possible outcomes are there? _____

13. What is the probability that the pizza will have thin crust? _____

14. What is the probability that the pizza will have onions? _____

15. What is the probability that the pizza will be thick crust and have mushrooms? _____

Lesson 7.1 Understanding Probability

An **experiment** is an activity in which results are observed. Each round of an experiment is called a **trial**, and the result of a trial is called an **outcome**. A set of one ore more outcomes is an **event**.

The **probability** of an event is a measure of the likelihood that the event will occur. This measure ranges from 0 to 1 and can be written as a ratio, fraction, decimal, or percent. To calculate probability, you must first know the number of possible outcomes.

The possible outcomes when you roll a die are the following: 1, 2, 3, 4, 5, and 6.

Every outcome is equally likely.

There is no chance that you can roll a 7.

Answer each question below based on the experiment described.

a	b

1. You flip a coin.

Possible outcomes?

heads, tails

Outcomes equally likely? (Yes or no)

yes

2. You roll a pair of dice and find the sum.

Possible outcomes?

_1, 2, 3, 4, 5, 6, 7, 8, 9, 10, 11, 12_

An impossible outcome?

_29_

3. A bowl contains 15 red marbles and 5 green marbles.

Possible outcomes?

green or red

Most likely outcome?

red

4. Twenty names are written on slips of paper in a basket.

Possible outcomes?

any of 20

Outcomes equally likely? (Yes or no)

yes

Lesson 7.2 Frequency Tables

A **frequency table** shows how often an item, a number, or a range of numbers occurs. The **cumulative frequency** is the sum of all frequencies up to and including the current one. The **relative frequency** is the percentage of a specific frequency.

Make a frequency table for these test scores:

71, 85, 73, 92, 86, 79, 87,

98, 82, 93, 81, 89, 88, 96

Test Scores

Score	Frequency	Cumulative Frequency	Relative Frequency
71–75	2	2	14.3%
76–80	1	3	7.1%
81–85	3	6	21.4%
86–90	4	10	28.6%
91–95	2	12	14.3%
96–100	2	14	14.3%

Use the following data to complete the frequency table.

1. Cats' weights (in pounds):

9.4375, 11.375, 12.1875,

11.625, 8.625, 9.6875,

8.875, 12.5, 9.375,

10.25, 10.625, 12.0625,

11.875, 8.9375, 9.75,

10.1875, 10.125, 10.1875,

12.0, 9.125

Cats' Weights

Weight (in pounds)	Frequency	Cumulative Frequency	Relative Frequency
8.6–8.99			%
9–9.5			%
9.6–9.99			%
10–10.5			%
10.6–10.99			%
11–11.5			%
11.6–11.99			%
12–12.5			%

Answer the following questions about the frequency table above.

2. How many cats weigh 12–12.5 pounds? _____

3. How many cats weigh 10.6–10.99 pounds? _____

4. How many cats weigh less than 10 pounds? _____

5. How many cats weigh 11 pounds or more? _____

6. What percentage of cats are 10–10.5 pounds? _____

7. What percentage of cats are less than 9 pounds? _____

Lesson 7.2 Frequency Tables

A frequency table can be created by looking at a data set, choosing ranges for examining the data, and calculating the frequency with which the data occurs in the set.

14, 15, 12, 15, 12, 13, 20, 15, 21, 25, 16, 18, 17, 21, 23, 16, 23, 19, 23, 22

Step 1: Choose the value ranges for the table.

Step 2: Find the frequency for each value range.

Step 3: Calculate the cumulative frequency by finding the sum of all frequencies up to and including the current one.

Values	Frequency	Cumulative Frequency	Relative Frequency
11–15	7	7	35%
16–20	6	13	30%
21–25	7	20	35%

Step 4: Find the relative frequency by calculating the percentage of the whole that is made up by each frequency.

Create a frequency table for each data set.

1. 6, 6, 5, 4, 6, 6, 8, 6, 3, 2, 4, 5, 6, 8, 8, 3, 3, 3, 4, 3

2. 24, 22, 26, 24, 25, 22, 21, 21

3. 8, 6, 8, 7, 7, 5, 8, 5, 5, 6, 8, 4, 2

Lesson 7.3   Calculating Probability

The **probability** of an event is the measure of how likely it is that the event will occur.

Probability (P) = $\dfrac{\text{number of favorable outcomes}}{\text{number of possible outcomes}}$

A bag contains 12 marbles, 7 blue and 5 red. If a marble is chosen at random, the probability that it will be red is:

Probability (P) = $\dfrac{5}{12}$ — the number of red marbles
— the total number of marbles

Solve each problem. Write answers as fractions in simplest form.

1. A bag contains 5 blue marbles, 3 red marbles, and 2 white marbles. What is the probability

    a selected marble will be red? 3/10

    What is the probability that a selected marble will not be white? 8/10 or ⁴/5

    What is the probability that a selected marble will be either blue or white? 7/10

Use the spinner to find the following probabilities. Write answers as fractions in simplest form.

2. $P(3)$ = 1/6

3. $P(\text{odd})$ = 1/2

4. $P(1 \text{ or } 4)$ = 2/6 or 1/3

5. $P(>4)$ = 1/3 or 2/6

6. $P(<6)$ = 5/6

7. $P(\text{not 5 or 3})$ = 4/6 or ²/3

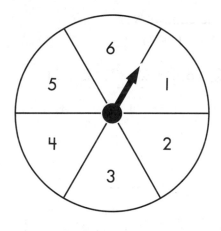

Lesson 7.3 Calculating Probability

Probability can also be thought of as the ratio of desired outcome(s) to the sample space. It can be expressed as a ratio, fraction, decimal, or percent.

When tossing a coin, what is the probability that it will land on heads?

desired outcome: heads   sample space: heads, tails   probability: 1:2, $\frac{1}{2}$, 50%, 0.5

Find the probability. Write answers as fractions in simplest form.

A box contains 3 red pencils, 4 blue pencils, 2 green pencils, and 1 regular pencil. If you take 1 pencil without looking, what is the probability of picking each of the following?

1. a red pencil _____

2. a blue pencil _____

3. a green pencil _____

4. a regular pencil _____

If you spin the spinner shown at the right, what is the probability of the spinner stopping on each of the following?

5. a letter _____

6. an odd number _____

7. an even number _____

8. a vowel _____

9. the number 3 _____

10. a consonant _____

Lesson 7.3 Calculating Probability

Determine the probability for each of the following events. Write answers as fractions in simplest form.

1. drawing a gray marble _____

2. drawing a white marble _____

3. drawing a black marble _____

4. drawing either a gray or a black marble _____

5. spinning a gray section _____

6. spinning a 4 _____

7. spinning a 1 _____

8. spinning *either* a 4 or 5 _____

9. spinning an even number _____

10. spinning a red section _____

11. spinning a blue section _____

12. spinning a yellow section _____

A jar contains 25 pennies, 20 nickels, and 15 dimes. If someone picks one coin without looking, what are the chances that they will pick the following:

13. penny _____

14. nickel _____

15. dime _____

Lesson 7.4 Uniform Probability Models

When all outcomes of an experiment are equally likely, the event has **uniform probability**.

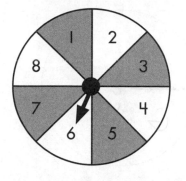

This spinner has 8 equally divided sections. Every time it is used, there is an equal chance ($\frac{1}{8}$) that it will land on any given number.

Chance of spinning 6 — $\frac{1}{8}$

Chance of spinning 3 — $\frac{1}{8}$

Chance of spinning 7 — $\frac{1}{8}$

Write *yes* or *no* to tell if each situation describes a uniform probability model.

	a	**b**
1.	rolling one die	rolling two dice
2.	flipping a coin	a spinner with 3 stars and 2 diamonds
3.	calling on a girl in class	calling on any student in class
4.	winning the lottery	drawing an 8 from a deck of cards
5.	calling on a boy in class	a spinner with 5 red and 2 blue sections
6.	flipping a coin and rolling a die	a spinner with 3 squares and 3 triangles

Lesson 7.4 Uniform Probability Models

When all outcomes of an experiment are equally likely, the event has **uniform probability**.

To create a uniform probability problem, divide the event into equal sections of different possibilities.

Color one section red. Color one section yellow. Color one section blue. Color one section green.

There is a $\frac{1}{4}$ chance of spinning red, blue, yellow, or green.

This is an example of a spinner that has uniform probability.

Follow the directions to set up uniform probabilities.

1. Draw a spinner that has an equal chance of spinning a star or a diamond.

2. Draw a spinner that has an equal chance of spinning a number 1 through 4.

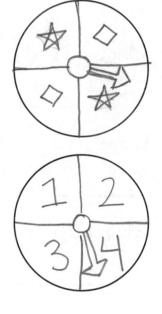

3. Color the marbles so that there is an equal chance of pulling a blue or green marble.

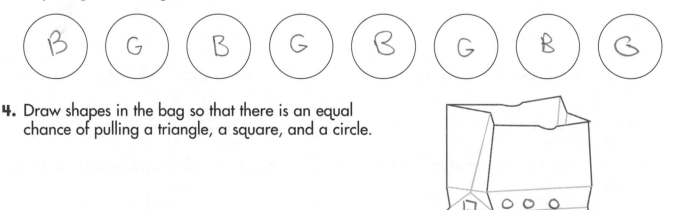

4. Draw shapes in the bag so that there is an equal chance of pulling a triangle, a square, and a circle.

Lesson 7.5 Other Probability Models

When an event does not have uniform probability, the odds of each particular outcome are not equally likely.

When using this spinner, there is a greater chance of landing in the blue section than there is of landing in the red or white sections.

Chance of spinning blue — $\frac{1}{2}$

Chance of spinning red — $\frac{1}{4}$

Chance of spinning white — $\frac{1}{4}$

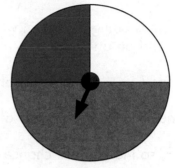

For each situation pictured, state if the odds of all outcomes are *equal* or *not equal*.

a   b

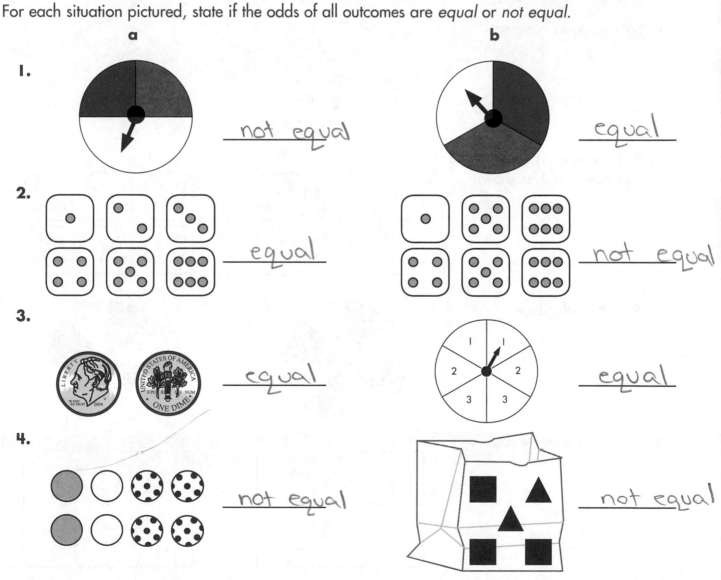

1. a. not equal   b. equal

2. a. equal   b. not equal

3. a. equal   b. equal

4. a. not equal   b. not equal

Lesson 7.5 Other Probability Models

When a probability event has unequal odds, they can be rated the same way as fractions or other ratios.

A game is being played in which the spinner must land on a star to win.

Spinner 1 — $\frac{2}{6}$ or $\frac{1}{3}$ chance of spinning a star

Spinner 2 — $\frac{3}{6}$ or $\frac{1}{2}$ chance of spinning a star

$\frac{1}{3} < \frac{1}{2}$, so the greatest chance of winning is using spinner 2.

Spinner 1 Spinner 2

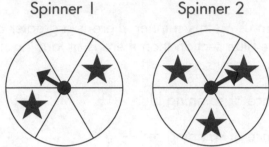

Circle the spinner with the best odds of winning. Show your work.

1. Spin an even number:

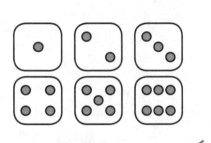

2. Roll a sum of 10 with two dice numbered as shown:

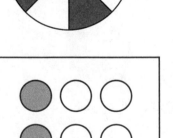

3. Spin the color blue.

4. Choose a gray marble.

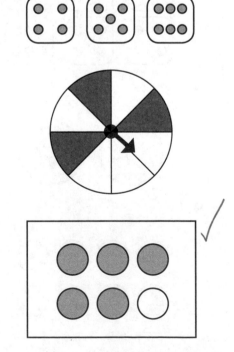

Lesson 7.5 Other Probability Models

Solve the problems below.

1. A spinner has 6 sections of equal size. One is red, two are blue, and 3 are yellow.

   a. If you spin the spinner one time, what are the odds that you will land on blue? _____

   b. If you spin the spinner twice, what are the odds that you will land on yellow on the

   second spin? _____

2. You flip a coin that has a heads side and a tails side.

   a. What are the odds that the coin will land on heads the first time you flip it? _____

   b. You have flipped the coin 50 times. You have landed on heads 31 times and
   tails 19 times. What are the odds that the coin will land on tails on the next flip? _____

3. At the school festival, you can win a bicycle by pulling a red ball out of bag. The first bag has
52 white balls, 27 green balls, and 11 red balls. The second bag has 25 white balls, 25
green balls, 25 yellow balls, and 10 red balls.

   a. What are the odds of pulling a red ball from the first bag? _____

   b. What are the odds of pulling a red ball from the second bag? _____

   c. Which bag has the best odds? _____

4. You roll two regular dice that are numbered 1–6. What is the probability of rolling the
following sums:

   a. 2: _____   **e.** 6: _____   **i.** 10: _____

   b. 3: _____   **f.** 7: _____   **j.** 11: _____

   c. 4: _____   **g.** 8: _____   **k.** 12: _____

   d. 5: _____   **h.** 9: _____

   Which sum gives you the best odds? _____

5. A bag contains 9 green marbles and 16 red marbles. You will choose one marble out of the
bag without looking.

   a. What are the odds of choosing a red marble? _____

   b. You do not replace marbles after they are chosen.
   So far you have chosen 4 red marbles and 2 green
   marbles. What are the odds of choosing a red marble now? _____

Lesson 7.6 Understanding Compound Events

The **Fundamental Counting Principle** states that when an experiment is conducted that is considered a **compound** event, or an event that has more than one element, the number of possible outcomes can be calculated by considering the number of possible outcomes for each element. The number of possible outcomes for the first element (a) can be multiplied by the number of possible outcomes for the second element (b) to find the total number of possible outcomes (o). So, $a \times b = o$.

There are 3 balls (yellow, red, and green) in one bag and 4 balls (purple, blue, white, and black) in another bag. If a person draws one ball from each bag, how many possible outcomes are there?

Step 1: Find the number of outcomes for the first event.   3

Step 2: Find the number of outcomes for the second event.   4

Step 3: Multiply these together. 3×4

Step 4: State the number of possible outcomes for the combined event.   12

Use the Fundamental Counting Principle to find the number of possible outcomes for each compound event described.

a

b

1. rolling two dice that are numbered 1–6

   _____

   flipping a coin and rolling a die numbered 1–6

   _____

2. spinning a 4-part spinner and flipping a coin

   _____

   pulling a card from a full deck and flipping a coin

   _____

3. spinning a 6-part spinner and rolling a die numbered 1–6

   _____

   flipping a coin and rolling two dice numbered 1–6

   _____

4. spinning a 4-part spinner and pulling a card from a full deck

   _____

   flipping 2 coins and rolling 2 dice numbered 1–6

   _____

Lesson 7.6 Understanding Compound Events SHOW YOUR WORK

Use the Fundamental Counting Principle to find the number of possible outcomes. Show your work.

1. 3 coins are tossed and two six-sided dice are rolled. How many possible outcomes are there?

There are _____ possible outcomes.

2. Jed is shopping. He is looking at 5 different ties, 3 different sweaters, and 4 different shirts. How many possible combinations can he make?

Jed can make _____ possible combinations.

3. Miranda's jewelry box contains 8 necklaces, 10 pairs of earrings, and 4 bracelets. How many combinations, which contain all 3 kinds of jewelry, can she make?

Miranda can make _____ combinations of jewelry.

4. Robert has to color in 4 different shapes (circle, square, triangle, and rectangle) and has 5 colors to choose from (green, yellow, red, blue, and orange). If he can only use each color one time, how many ways can he color the shapes?

Robert can color the shapes _____ different ways.

5. Spencer needs to put on gloves, a hat, and a scarf. He has 5 hats, 4 pairs of gloves, and 9 scarves to choose from. How many combinations of gloves, hat, and scarf can Spencer make?

Spencer can make _____ combinations.

6. Pilar wants to cook a meal that consists of a meat, a starch, and a vegetable. At the grocery store there are 8 choices of meat, 8 choices of vegetables, and 3 choices of starches. How many possible combinations can Pilar make?

Pilar can make _____ combinations.

7. Jacob must collect a flower, a vegetable, and an herb. In the garden, there are 10 kinds of flowers, 7 kinds of vegetables, and 4 kinds of herbs. How many combinations can Jacob make?

Jacob can make _____ combinations.

1.

2.

3.

4.

5.

6.

7.

Lesson 7.7 Representing Compound Events

A **sample space** is a set of all possible outcomes (or possible results) for an activity or experiment. To determine the sample space, it is helpful to organize the possibilities using a list, chart, picture, or tree diagram.

Show the sample space for tossing a nickel, a dime, and a quarter.

Nickel	Dime	Quarter	Possible Outcomes	
Heads (H)	H	H	HHH	There are 8 possible outcomes
		T	HHT	or possible results.
	T	H	HTH	
		T	HTT	
Tails (T)	H	H	THH	
		T	THT	
	T	H	TTH	
		T	TTT	

Make a tree diagram for each situation. Determine the number of possible outcomes.

1. The concession stand offers the drink choices shown in the table.

Drinks	Sizes
Lemonade	Small
Fruit Punch	Medium
Apple Cider	Large
	Jumbo

There are _____ possible outcomes.

2. The Kellys are planning their vacation activities. The first day they can go to the zoo or the museum. The second day they can go to the pier or the dunes. The third day they have to choose sailing, swimming, or horseback riding.

There are _____ possible outcomes.

Lesson 7.7 Representing Compound Events

One way to show sample space for compound events is with a chart. What is the sample space if you roll 1 die and flip 1 coin?

Chart

Penny

	Heads	Tails
1	H1	T1
2	H2	T2
3	H3	T3
4	H4	T4
5	H5	T5
6	H6	T6

Die

What is the sample space? It is 12, because there are 12 possible outcomes.

Solve each problem.

1. Juan flips a penny, a nickel, and a dime at the same time. How many different combinations of heads and tails can he get?

_____

2. Latisha has red, blue, and black sneakers; blue, tan, and white pants; and black and gray sweatshirts. How many different outfits can she make?

_____

3. Jonathan, Kaitlin, and Ling are trying to decide in what order they should appear during their talent show performance. They made this chart showing the possible orders. Can you show the same results using a tree diagram? (Remember, each person can appear only once in the 1, 2, 3 order.) What is the total number of possible orders?

_____

1	2	3
J	K	L
K	L	J
L	K	J
J	L	K
K	J	L
L	J	K

Lesson 7.7 Representing Compound Events

Tables can be used to represent compound events that have two elements.

John rolls two dice. What is the probability that he will roll a sum of nine?

Step 1: Create a table with rows that match one part of the event and columns that match the other part of the event.

Step 2: Fill in the headers for your table with the possible outcomes for each part of the event.

Step 3: Fill in the table with the possible final outcomes.

Step 4: Find the total number of possible final outcomes (36) and the number of final outcomes with the desired characteristic (4) to calculate the probability.

Possible Outcomes Die #2

Possible Outcomes Die #1

	1	2	3	4	5	6
1	2	3	4	5	6	7
2	3	4	5	6	7	8
3	4	5	6	7	8	9
4	5	6	7	8	9	10
5	6	7	8	9	10	11
6	7	8	9	10	11	12

The shaded numbers are the final outcomes, or sums when the outcomes are added together.

The probability is $\frac{4}{36}$, or $\frac{1}{9}$.

Create a table to solve the problems.

1. Erin is getting dressed in the morning. She is choosing from 4 skirts (black, brown, blue, and khaki) and 5 sweaters (black, blue, red, green, and yellow). What is the probability that she will wear both black and blue?

2. Michael is playing a game in which you spin a spinner numbered 1–8 first, and then roll a die numbered 1–6. What is the probability that he will spin and roll a sum of 10?

Lesson 7.8 Problem Solving

Solve each problem. Use either the Fundamental Counting Principle, a tree diagram, or a table to solve each problem. Show your work.

1. Stephen flips a coin and pulls a marble from a bag which contains equal amounts of red, green, yellow, and blue marbles. How many outcomes are possible?

   There are _____ possible outcomes.

   Which strategy did you use to solve this problem?

   _____

2. Julie is playing a game. She has a bag with cards numbered 1–10 and another bag with red and yellow bouncy balls. She pulls a number card out of one bag and a bouncy ball out of another bag. How many outcomes are possible?

   There are _____ possible outcomes.

   Which strategy did you use to solve this problem?

   _____

3. At the sandwich shop, Nick can order a sandwich on a sub roll, wheat bread, or a Kaiser roll. He can have ham, turkey, or roast beef. Then, he can add cheese, lettuce, or pickles. What is the probability that he will have a sandwich that is both on wheat bread and made with ham?

   There is a _____ chance of his ordering a sandwich with both wheat bread and ham.

   Which strategy did you use to solve this problem?

   _____

4. Jeff has a deck of cards and a coin. What is the chance that he will pull a 10 from the deck of cards and land on heads?

   There is a _____ chance of Jeff pulling a 10 and flipping heads at the same time?

   Which strategy did you use to solve this problem?

   _____

1.

2.

3.

4.

Lesson 7.8 Problem Solving

SHOW YOUR WORK

Solve each problem. Use the Fundamental Counting Principle, a tree diagram, or a table to solve each problem. Show your work.

1. Mark and his friends are playing a game. They take turns pulling a number 1–5 out of one bag and a number 6–10 out of another bag. They keep their score and then put the numbers back. The first person to get a sum of 15 wins. What is the probability of winning on each turn?

   There is a _____ chance of winning the game on each turn.

   Which strategy did you use to solve this problem?

   _____

2. Mr. Roberts' son has a set of blocks that are made up of 12 different shapes and 4 different colors. Every shape comes in every color. How many blocks are in the set?

   There are _____ blocks in the set.

   Which strategy did you use to solve this problem?

   _____

3. Sarah is at the smoothie shop. She can choose a base of ice, banana, or yogurt. She can add blueberries, strawberries, or mangoes. Then, she can add honey, protein powder, or kale. How many combinations are possible?

   Sarah has _____ combinations to choose from.

   Which strategy did you use to solve this problem?

   _____

4. A box of chocolates is half milk chocolate and half dark chocolate. Each kind of chocolate is filled with coconut, caramel, nuts, or cherries. What is the probability of choosing a candy that is made of dark chocolate and cherries?

   There is a _____ chance of choosing a candy made of dark chocolate and cherries.

   Which strategy did you use to solve this problem?

   _____

1.

2.

3.

4.

Lesson 7.8 Problem Solving

SHOW YOUR WORK

Solve each problem. Use the Fundamental Counting Principle, a tree diagram, or a table to solve each problem. Show your work.

1. A cube with six sides has the letters A–F on it. A spinner has the letters G–L on it. How many letter combinations are there when the cube is rolled and the spinner is spun?

   There are _____ possible letter combinations.

   Which strategy did you use to solve this problem?

   _____

2. A bakery has both donuts and bagels. They are each available in blueberry, chocolate, and plain. What is the probability of choosing at random a blueberry bagel?

   There is a _____ chance of randomly choosing a blueberry bagel.

   Which strategy did you use to solve this problem?

   _____

3. Customers have a choice of thin crust, hand-tossed crust, or deep dish pizzas. They can add a pesto, tomato, or olive oil base. Finally, they can add pepperoni, mushrooms, or onions. What is the probability that a customer will order a pizza with both thin crust and mushrooms?

   There is a _____ chance that a customer will order a pizza with both thin crust and mushrooms.

   Which strategy did you use to solve this problem?

   _____

4. Katie is trying to decide where to go on vacation. She has narrowed it down to Spain, Hawaii, and Puerto Rico. She can take between 7 and 10 days for her trip. How many options does she have?

   Katie has _____ choices for her vacation.

   Which strategy did you use to solve this problem?

   _____

1.

2.

3.

4.

Check What You Learned

Probability

Fill in the missing data in the frequency table. Then, answer the questions.

Scores on Last Week's Quiz

	Score Range	Frequency	Cumulative Frequency	Relative Frequency
1.	(0–5)		3	$\frac{1}{8}$
2.	(6–10)		7	$\frac{1}{6}$
3.	(11–15)		16	$\frac{3}{8}$
4.	(16–20)		24	$\frac{1}{3}$

5. How many students' scores were included in the table? _____

6. Which score range was most frequent? _____

7. What was the relative frequency of a score between 16 and 20? _____

Make a frequency table for the data below.

Cars Across the Bridge Per Day — 93, 105, 92, 111, 98, 97, 108, 101, 112, 115, 96, 104, 103, 91, 97

8.

Use the spinner to answer the questions.

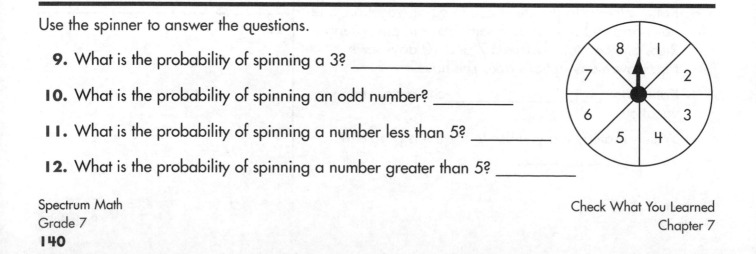

9. What is the probability of spinning a 3? _____

10. What is the probability of spinning an odd number? _____

11. What is the probability of spinning a number less than 5? _____

12. What is the probability of spinning a number greater than 5? _____

Check What You Learned

Probability

Create a tree diagram using the situation described below and use it to answer the questions.

13. Paul is getting a new bike. He can get either a racing bike or a mountain bike. His color choices are red, black, and silver. Make a tree diagram showing Paul's possible outcomes.

14. How many possible outcomes are there? _____

15. What is the probability that Paul will get a racing bike? _____

16. What is the probability that the bike will be red? _____

17. What is the probability that Paul will get a silver mountain bike? _____

Color or label the shapes below to set up an event with uniform probability.

18.

19.

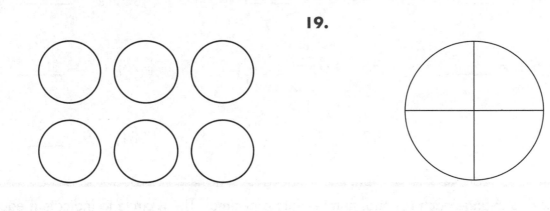

20. Drew and Haley are going out to dinner. At the restaurant, each person orders an appetizer, an entrée, a dessert, and a drink. On the menu there are 7 choices of appetizers, 15 choices of entrées, 6 choices of desserts, and 5 choices of drinks. How many combinations can Drew make for his meal at the restaurant?

Drew can make _____ combinations for his meal.

Final Test Chapters 1–7

Add, subtract, multiply, or divide.

	a	b	c
1.	$3 + (-7) =$ _____	$2\frac{1}{4} + 2\frac{2}{3} =$ _____	$(-5) + 8 =$ _____
2.	$(-8) + 12 =$ _____	$9 + (-11) =$ _____	$(-7) + 2 =$ _____
3.	$5 - 8 =$ _____	$6 - 5 =$ _____	$|-2| - 8 =$ _____
4.	$3\frac{3}{10} - 2\frac{4}{5} =$ _____	$(-6) - 5 =$ _____	$5 - 6 =$ _____
5.	$(23) \times (-3) =$ _____	$45 \times 8 =$ _____	$(-18) \times (-6) =$ _____
6.	$71 \times (-5) =$ _____	$(-83) \times 7 =$ _____	$\frac{4}{5} \times \frac{1}{8} =$ _____
7.	$(-24) \div (-4) =$ _____	$45 \div (-9) =$ _____	$(-95) \div 5 =$ _____
8.	$(-22) \div (-1) =$ _____	$42 \div (-7) =$ _____	$(-81) \div 9 =$ _____

Use long division to change each rational number into a decimal. Then, circle to indicate if each is terminating (T) or repeating (R).

	a	b	c
9.	$\frac{3}{5} =$ _____ T or R	$\frac{7}{50} =$ _____ T or R	$\frac{1}{125} =$ _____ T or R

CHAPTERS 1–7 FINAL TEST

Spectrum Math
Grade 7
142

Final Test
Chapters 1–7

Final Test Chapters 1–7

Solve each problem. Use 3.14 for π when needed.

10. 331 students went on a field trip. Six buses were filled and 7 students traveled in cars. How many students were in each bus?

Let s represent the number of students on each bus.

Equation: _____

There were _____ students on each bus.

10.

11. The length of a football field is 30 yards more than its width. If it is 100 yards long, how wide is the field?

Let w represent the width of the field.

Equation: _____

The football field is _____ yards wide.

11.

12. Julia has 3 red marbles, 4 blue marbles, 3 yellow marbles, and 6 black marbles. She takes one marble out of the bag at random.

The probability that it is a black marble is _____.

The probability that it is a yellow marble is _____.

The probability that it is not a red marble is _____.

12.

13. The municipal swimming pool is 50 meters long and 25 meters wide, and it is filled to a uniform depth of 3 meters. What is the volume of water in the pool?

The volume of the water is _____ cubic meters.

13.

14. There are four hundred students at Thompson Middle School. If 54% of the students are female, what is the ratio of female students to male students?

The ratio of female to male students is _____.

14.

15. Ben is putting in a 7-foot diameter circular flower bed at his school. He wants to put plastic edging along the outside edge of the flower bed. How much edging will he need?

Ben will need _____ feet of plastic edging.

15.

Spectrum Math
Grade 7

CHAPTERS 1–7 FINAL TEST

Final Test
Chapters 1–7
143

Final Test Chapters 1–7

Write *yes* or *no* to tell if each set of ratios is proportional.

	a	**b**	**c**	**d**
16.	$\frac{5}{4}, \frac{35}{28}$	$\frac{4}{3}, \frac{24}{30}$	$\frac{6}{5}, \frac{24}{20}$	$\frac{11}{3}, \frac{33}{9}$
	_____	_____		_____

Find the constant of proportionality for the set of values.

17.

x	7.5	10	17.5	20
y	4.5	6	10.5	12

$k =$ _____

These similar triangles are drawn to scale. Find the missing side lengths.

a

18.

$AC =$ _____ cm

$DF =$ _____ cm

$FE =$ _____ cm

b

$ST =$ _____ ft.

$TU =$ _____ ft.

$VX =$ _____ ft.

Find the area of each figure and the area and circumference of each circle. Use 3.14 for π. Round answers to the nearest hundredth.

	a	**b**	**c**
19.			

circumference: _____ cm   _____ in.   _____ yd.

area: _____ sq. cm   _____ sq. in.   _____ sq. yd.

20.

$A =$ _____ in.^{2}

$A =$ _____ m^2

$A =$ _____ ft.^{2}

Final Test Chapters 1–7

Answer the questions about the angles below. ∠M = 55°, ∠X = 35°

21. ∠Y = _____

22. ∠Z = _____

23. ∠W = _____

24. ∠N = _____

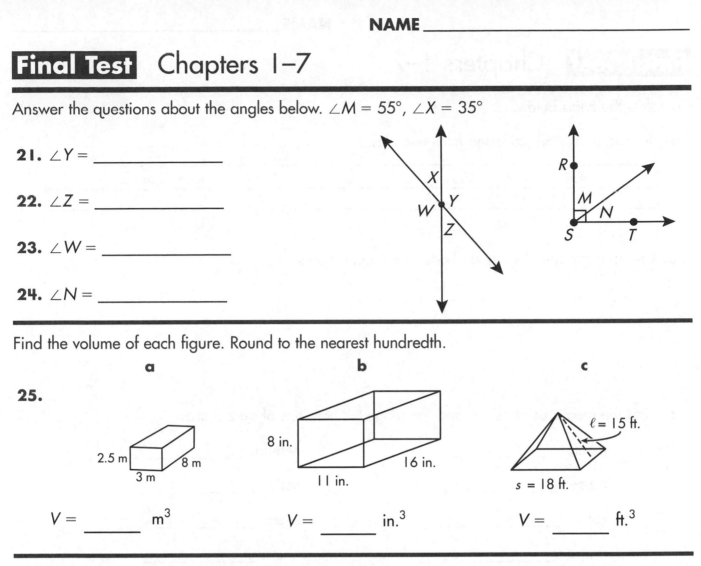

Find the volume of each figure. Round to the nearest hundredth.

a	b	c

25.

2.5 m   3 m   8 m

8 in.   11 in.   16 in.

ℓ = 15 ft.   s = 18 ft.

$V =$ _____ m^3

$V =$ _____ in.^{3}

$V =$ _____ ft.^{3}

Create a tree diagram using the situation described below and use it to answer the questions.

26. Tracy decides to visit the concession stand while she is at the movies. She wants a drink, popcorn, and candy. She can choose between a cola, juice, and water to drink. She can top her popcorn with butter or have it plain. Finally, she has a choice of chocolate mints, red licorice, or caramels for her candy. Make a tree diagram that shows all possible combinations.

27. What is the total number of possible outcomes? _____

28. What is probability of having red licorice? _____

29. What is the probability of having buttered popcorn and caramels? _____

Spectrum Math
Grade 7

Final Test
Chapters 1–7

145

CHAPTERS 1–7 FINAL TEST

Final Test Chapters 1–7

Complete the items below.

Sample quiz scores are collected from two classes.

Quiz Scores — Class 1	Quiz Scores — Class 2
9, 18, 12, 9, 13, 22, 8, 23, 16, 17	22, 20, 22, 15, 10, 17, 21, 23, 14, 11
a	**b**

30. Create a graphic display for both sets of quiz scores.

31. Find the measures of center and the range for both sets of quiz scores.

median: _____   median: _____

mode: _____   mode: _____

mean: _____   mean: _____

range: _____   range: _____

32. If there are 30 students in Class 1, what is the best prediction
for the number of students who scored a 10 or less on the quiz? _____

33. If there are 25 students in Class 2, what is the best prediction
for the number of students who scored more than 20 on the quiz? _____

34. Tell one way the two data sets are alike and different.

alike: _____   different: _____

Tell which property is used in each equation (*commutative*, *associative*, or *identity*).

a	**b**

35. $5 + 3 = 3 + 5$ _____ $0 + 8 = 8$ _____

36. $(2 + 1) + 5 = 2 + (1 + 5)$ _____ $-5 + 5 = 0$ _____

Spectrum Math
Grade 7
146

Final Test
Chapters 1–7

CHAPTERS 1–7 FINAL TEST

Scoring Record for Posttests, Mid-Tests, and Final Test

Chapter Posttest	Your Score	Performance			
		Excellent	Very Good	Fair	Needs Improvement
1	____ of 46	41–46	37–40	32–36	31 or fewer
2	____ of 32	29–32	26–28	23–25	22 or fewer
3	____ of 30	27–30	24–26	21–23	20 or fewer
4	____ of 23	22–23	19–21	15–18	14 or fewer
5	____ of 21	19–21	17–18	15–16	14 or fewer
6	____ of 26	24–26	21–23	19–20	18 or fewer
7	____ of 20	18–20	16–17	14–15	13 or fewer
Mid-Test	____ of 79	72–79	65–71	56–64	55 or fewer
Final Test	____ of 93	85–93	75–84	66–74	65 or fewer

Record your test score in the Your Score column. See where your score falls in the Performance columns. Your score is based on the total number of required responses. If your score is fair or needs improvement, review the chapter material.

Grade 7 Answers

Chapter 1

Pretest, page 5

	a	b	c
1.	-45	9	10
2.	-21	-6	31
3.	-52	89	-18
4.	7	34	58
5.	-35	-56	39
6.	identity		
7.	commutative		
8.	associative		
9.	associative	identity	
10.	commutative	commutative	
11.	identity	associative	
12.	identity	commutative	

Pretest, page 6

	a	b	c	d
13.	$4\frac{11}{12}$	$5\frac{9}{14}$	$6\frac{19}{24}$	$4\frac{18}{35}$
14.	$4\frac{1}{12}$	$\frac{1}{8}$	$2\frac{1}{2}$	$2\frac{1}{14}$
15.	-1	1	3	
16.	-11	-1	-13	
17.	-6	7	-6	
18.	$10\frac{1}{24}$			
19.	$26\frac{1}{6}$			
20.	$6\frac{1}{4}$			

Lesson 1.1, page 7

	a	b	c
1.	-19	7	2
2.	-28	50	-10
3.	-92	31	74
4.	-936	-76	-65
5.	32	36	-73
6.	-55	47	-87
7.	61	-37	23
8.	-25	-68	53
9.	-71	99	-90
10.	-40	-44	77
11.	52	-66	95
12.	-15	20	9

Lesson 1.2, page 8

	a	b	c
1.	91	19	9
2.	1	199	0
3.	762	78	302
4.	4002	-668	-8701
5.	23	56	-432
6.	53	694	-274
7.	516	883	-637
8.	413	590	739
9.	281	40	-826
10.	206	372	973
11.	-533	836	954
12.	344	-711	219

Lesson 1.3, page 9

	a	b
1.	8 + (-3)	9 + (-2)
2.	12 – 7	8 – 12
3.	52 + (-13)	23 + (-10)
4.	67 – 11	45 – 6
5.	30 + (-15)	74 + (-23)
6.	3 – 56	62 – 32
7.	87 + (-85)	54 + (-20)
8.	50 – 17	41 – 12
9.	89 + (-57)	46 + (-40)
10.	96 – 20	94 – 90
11.	83 + (-67)	98 + (-34)
12.	76 – 20	90 – 76

Lesson 1.4, page 10

	a	b	c	d
1.	$1\frac{3}{8}$	$\frac{5}{6}$	$1\frac{3}{20}$	$\frac{1}{2}$
2.	$1\frac{7}{40}$	$\frac{4}{5}$	$\frac{11}{12}$	$1\frac{9}{20}$
3.	$\frac{5}{8}$	$\frac{29}{35}$	$1\frac{1}{56}$	$\frac{13}{15}$
4.	$3\frac{7}{12}$	$10\frac{7}{8}$	$6\frac{13}{21}$	$4\frac{7}{10}$
5.	$7\frac{7}{9}$	$2\frac{33}{40}$	$5\frac{19}{24}$	$3\frac{22}{35}$
6.	$5\frac{3}{4}$	$4\frac{7}{18}$	$4\frac{47}{70}$	$6\frac{5}{6}$

Lesson 1.5, page 11

	a	b	c	d
1.	7	-7	-1	1
2.	-6	0	0	6
3.	4	-4	-6	6
4.	-4	-10	4	10
5.	11	-3	3	-11
6.	0	-16	16	0
7.	-3	3	-11	1
8.	-1	11	-8	8
9.	3	-9	9	-3
10.	-10	-2	2	10

Lesson 1.5, page 12

	a	b	c
1.	8	5	-2
2.	3	-9	-1
3.	-16	-11	2
4.	-9	1	-1
5.	0	-3	-10
6.	-24	85	58
7.	-12	21	0
8.	-24	9	-6
9.	48	-15	-11
10.	9	-8	-9

Lesson 1.6, page 13

	a	b	c
1.	-8	3	-10
2.	-15	1	-5
3.	-15	-10	43
4.	0	-11	-4
5.	7	9	-16
6.	28	12	14

7.	-15	-1	-21
8.	15	16	3
9.	-27	-55	-3
10.	-45	3	37

Lesson 1.6, page 14

	a	b	c
1.	-5	-29	48
2.	44	-57	43
3.	17	73	6
4.	-68	-65	-18
5.	-3	-65	-10
6.	18	-11	-1
7.	25	34	56
8.	-72	12	43
9.	73	-4	26
10.	-69	80	25
11.	-14	-58	75
12.	77	-45	41
13.	62	35	-80
14.	-93	-102	-37

Lesson 1.7, page 15

	a	b	c	d
1.	$\frac{7}{20}$	$\frac{1}{5}$	$\frac{3}{8}$	$\frac{7}{15}$
2.	$\frac{1}{2}$	$\frac{7}{15}$	$\frac{11}{24}$	$\frac{1}{5}$
3.	$\frac{1}{12}$	$\frac{1}{18}$	$\frac{1}{6}$	$\frac{41}{99}$
4.	$1\frac{11}{72}$	$1\frac{11}{12}$	$\frac{3}{4}$	$1\frac{43}{56}$
5.	$1\frac{49}{88}$	$4\frac{4}{15}$	$2\frac{5}{6}$	$1\frac{23}{42}$
6.	$2\frac{1}{9}$	$1\frac{9}{20}$	$2\frac{17}{24}$	$1\frac{3}{8}$

Lesson 1.8, page 16

	a	b
1.	$n + 17$	n
2.	$x + (y + 2)$	$s + r$
3.	x	$3 + (g + h)$
4.	$9 + (r + 5)$	$h + t$
5.	41	8
6.	45	19
7.	72	9
8.	116	18
9.	identity	commutative
10.	associative	identity
11.	associative	commutative
12.	identity	commutative

Lesson 1.9, page 17

1.	$\frac{3}{4}$
2.	$13\frac{31}{40}$
3.	$9\frac{7}{12}$
4.	$\frac{3}{4}$
5.	$3\frac{31}{56}; 1\frac{17}{56}$
6.	$2\frac{11}{24}$

Lesson 1.9, page 18

1.	$1\frac{11}{12}$
2.	$\frac{1}{12}$
3.	1055.4
4.	$\frac{5}{24}$
5.	6.8
6.	212.8

Posttest, page 19

	a	b	c
1.	54	-19	-31
2.	6	-21	10
3.	-54	34	-86
4.	35	-43	35
5.	-75	-83	-99
6.	commutative		
7.	associative		
8.	identity		
9.	commutative	identity	
10.	associative	commutative	
11.	identity	associative	
12.	commutative	associative	

Posttest, page 20

	a	b	c	d
13.	$2\frac{5}{56}$	$5\frac{7}{12}$	$4\frac{17}{24}$	$7\frac{1}{8}$
14.	$3\frac{5}{12}$	$\frac{3}{8}$	$2\frac{31}{70}$	$2\frac{5}{12}$
15.	-2	4	-7	
16.	3	-3	-12	
17.	-3	17	-10	
18.	$2\frac{1}{24}$			
19.	$4\frac{1}{6}$			
20.	$5\frac{7}{12}$			

Chapter 2

Pretest, page 21

	a	b
1.	$x \times (3 + 7)$	$(8 \times b) + (8 \times 12)$
2.	$(4 \times 3) + (4 \times c)$	$5 \times (m + n)$
3.	identity	
4.	commutative	
5.	zero	
6.	associative	
7.	zero	associative
8.	identity	commutative
9.	0.6	0.5
10.	0.25	0.7

Grade 7 Answers

Pretest, page 22

	a	b	c
11.	$\frac{3}{10}$	$\frac{3}{14}$	$3\frac{15}{28}$
12.	$2\frac{55}{144}$	$\frac{11}{24}$	$3\frac{13}{14}$
13.	-12	-18	16
14.	-2	-4	10
15.	$3\frac{1}{4}$		
16.	$6; \frac{3}{7}$		
17.	$13\frac{3}{4}$		
18.	$612\frac{5}{8}$		

Lesson 2.1, page 23

	a	b
1.	$a \times (4 + 3)$	$(b \times 6) + (b \times 12)$
2.	$(4 \times a) + (4 \times b)$	$3 \times (a + b)$
3.	$d \times (5 - 2)$	$(5 \times 8) + (5 \times p)$
4.	$(d \times 8) - (d \times h)$	$(12 \times s) - (12 \times 10)$
5.	$(r \times 16) + (r \times s)$	$35 \times (t + y)$
6.	$8 \times (a + b)$	$(r \times q) - (r \times s)$
7.	$6 \times (12 - w)$	$(p \times 15) + (p \times z)$
8.	$(15 \times y) + (15 \times 0)$	$d \times (d + b)$
9.	$a \times (2 + 3 + 4)$	$(p \times a) + (p \times b) + (p \times 4)$
10.	$a \times (b + c - d)$	$(8 \times a) + (8 \times b) + (8 \times c)$

Lesson 2.2, page 24

	a	b	c	d
1.	$\frac{3}{8}$	$\frac{8}{15}$	$\frac{9}{16}$	$\frac{1}{10}$
2.	$\frac{21}{40}$	$\frac{1}{5}$	$\frac{3}{35}$	$\frac{6}{25}$
3.	$\frac{15}{64}$	$\frac{1}{3}$	$\frac{5}{9}$	$\frac{4}{21}$
4.	$3\frac{6}{7}$	$7\frac{1}{2}$	$3\frac{11}{18}$	$13\frac{1}{2}$
5.	$6\frac{11}{24}$	$2\frac{6}{7}$	$31\frac{1}{2}$	$17\frac{1}{2}$
6.	$94\frac{7}{8}$	$2\frac{2}{9}$	$3\frac{25}{48}$	$4\frac{1}{2}$

Lesson 2.3, page 25

	a	b	c	d
1.	6	-24	-24	12
2.	-56	-30	24	-44
3.	-32	4	-88	70
4.	40	-36	26	-81
5.	-17	-10	-42	35
6.	0	21	-60	15
7.	-16	40	-30	15
8.	-36	40	-40	45
9.	0	121	6	48
10.	24	20	36	28

Lesson 2.3, page 26

	a	b	c
1.	8	-9	144
2.	-63	72	-48
3.	-10	28	-30

4.	-2	-22	36
5.	22	77	-84
6.	40	77	-6
7.	-12	-36	12
8.	14	24	-21
9.	18	-64	10
10.	54	-32	-30
11.	384	-98	76
12.	-451	132	-324
13.	-506	84	-65
14.	-432	-396	552

Lesson 2.4, page 27

	a	b	c	d
1.	$5\frac{1}{4}$	$2\frac{8}{15}$	$1\frac{1}{2}$	$21\frac{1}{3}$
2.	$11\frac{2}{3}$	$1\frac{9}{16}$	$2\frac{6}{7}$	$\frac{3}{5}$
3.	$11\frac{1}{4}$	$\frac{3}{5}$	$3\frac{1}{3}$	$2\frac{1}{6}$
4.	10	$10\frac{15}{16}$	51	98
5.	$2\frac{1}{45}$	$1\frac{47}{63}$	$\frac{4}{5}$	$\frac{14}{15}$

Lesson 2.5, page 28

	a	b
1.	$-9; 18 = -9 \times (-2)$	$-7; -7 = -7 \times 1$
2.	$-5; 20 = -4 \times (-5)$	$14; -84 = -6 \times 14$
3.	$-5; 15 = -3 \times (-5)$	$6; -54 = -9 \times 6$
4.	$-5; -25 = 5 \times (-5)$	$3; -39 = -13 \times 3$
5.	$-9; 81 = (-9) \times (-9)$	$-12; -48 = 4 \times (-12)$
6.	$-9; -72 = 8 \times (-9)$	$-3; 36 = -12 \times (-3)$
7.	$-2; 22 = (-11) \times (-2)$	$-3; 18 = -6 \times (-3)$

Lesson 2.6, page 29

	a	b	c
1.	3	-4	-2
2.	-7	-2	-4
3.	-27	-7	11
4.	-3	-19	19
5.	-1	-2	6
6.	10	-3	5
7.	-16	17	-9
8.	-17	-9	16
9.	14	-10	-2
10.	-16	15	-6

Lesson 2.6, page 30

	a	b	c
1.	14	-14	16
2.	13	15	-18
3.	-20	-3	-3
4.	-20	-14	6
5.	8	-5	18
6.	-18	-15	-9
7.	7	11	16
8.	-6	-18	-16
9.	7	-2	-18
10.	17	2	11
11.	16	-12	15
12.	-8	-13	6
13.	13	-62	8

Grade 7 Answers

14.	61	86	-24

Lesson 2.7, page 31

	a	b
1.	associative	identity
2.	commutative	zero
3.	zero	associative
4.	$z \times 15$	0
5.	$12a$	$(14 \times 3) \times p$
6.	0	$6 \times (4 \times n)$

Lesson 2.8, page 32

	a	b	c
1.	0.25; T	2.6; T	0.625; T
2.	0.6; T	0.035; T	0.2424; R
3.	0.5454; R	0.14; T	4.136; T
4.	0.35; T	0.009009; R	0.008; T

Lesson 2.8, page 33

	a	b	c
1.	0.4	$0.\overline{6}$	0.5
2.	0.375	$0.\overline{18}$	$0.\overline{428571}$
3.	$0.1\overline{6}$	$0.\overline{66}$	0.5
4.	0.25	0.8	0.3
5.	0.6	$0.\overline{714285}$	$0.\overline{1818}$
6.	0.1	$0.8\overline{3}$	0.5

Lesson 2.9, page 34

1. $\dfrac{2}{3}$

2. $14\dfrac{7}{12}$

3. 5

4. $\dfrac{1}{4}$

5. $3\dfrac{1}{3}$

6. $14\dfrac{5}{8}$

7. $74\dfrac{2}{3}$

Lesson 2.9, page 35

1. $\dfrac{1}{10}$

2. $\dfrac{3}{32}$

3. $5\dfrac{7}{12}$

4. $0.83 or \dfrac{29}{35}$ of a dollar

5. $16 \left(16\dfrac{1}{2}\right)$

6. $3\dfrac{1}{8}$

7. $11.99

Posttest, page 36

	a	b
1.	$(7 \times 10) + (7 \times a)$	$2 \times (c + d)$
2.	$y \times (2 + 6)$	$(5 \times k) + (5 \times 4)$
3.	associative	
4.	zero	

5.	identity	
6.	commutative	
7.	commutative	associative
8.	identity	zero
9.	$0.\overline{22}$	$0.\overline{44}$
10.	$0.\overline{09}$	0.4

Posttest, page 37

	a	b	c
11.	$\dfrac{1}{8}$	$\dfrac{10}{21}$	$6\dfrac{7}{8}$
12.	$3\dfrac{9}{11}$	$\dfrac{23}{42}$	$2\dfrac{1}{2}$
13.	-42	-12	10
14.	-3	3	-3
15.	$6\dfrac{1}{2}$		
16.	$21\dfrac{2}{3}$		
17.	$10\dfrac{7}{8}$		
18.	$4\dfrac{2}{5}$		

Chapter 3

Pretest, page 38

	a	b
1.	$5 + (6 + 7)$	56
2.	0	9×8
3.	$(3 \times 5) - (3 \times 2)$	$7 \times (2 \times 3)$
4.	$n - 5$	$8 + n$
5.	$n \div 6$	$2 \times n$
6.	$3 + n = 12$	$n - 6 = 19$
7.	$30 \div n = 3$	$5 \times n = 15$
8.	$5 \times a$	$6 + h = 16$
9.	$x - 19$	$27 \div b = 9$
10.	$c - 12 = 5$	$6 \times k = 72$

Pretest, page 39

11. $1.50 \times p \le 22.00; 14
12. $n + (n + 1) + (n + 2) = 51$; 16
13. $(b + 8) \div 2 = 20$; 32
14. $(c \div 2) + 15 = 30$; 30
15. $(p + 5) \div 2 = 16$; 27

Lesson 3.1, page 40

	a	b
1.	$7 + (6 + y)$	724
2.	$8 \times z$	0
3.	$(6 \times a) + (6 \times b)$	0
4.	$y + 7$	$(5 \times 6) \times 3$
5.	45	$7 \times (3 + 7)$

Lesson 3.1, page 41

	a	b
1.	$3 + d$	$8 \times w$
2.	$12 - 7$	$2 + n = 9$
3.	$n \div 6 = 8$	$9 + 15$
4.	$5 + 6 = 11$	$12 \div s = 4$
5.	$t - 3 = 5$	$2 \times b = 4$
6.	$5 \times 3 = y$	$20 \div n = 5$
7.	$20 + 12$	$4 + 11 = 15$

8. $30 \div f = 3$ $7 \times b = 63$

Lesson 3.2, page 42

	a	b
1.	$n - (0.07 \times n)$	$9 \times (7 + n)$
	$n \times 0.93$	$(9 \times 7) + (9 \times n)$
2.	$\$25 + (\$25 \times 0.05)$	$n + 4n$
	$\$25 \times 1.05$	$5n$
3.	$a \div 5 = 9$	$k + \frac{1}{5}$
	$9 \times 5 = a$	$k + 0.2$
4.	$12(15 - c)$	$\$44 + (\$44 \times .20)$
	$(15 - c) \times 12$	$\$44 \times 1.2$
5.	$(7 + x) \times 10$	$h - 3\frac{1}{4}$
	$10 \times (7 + x)$	$h - 3.25$

Lesson 3.3, page 43

1. $d = (4 \times 40) - (4 \times 32)$
$d = 4 \times (40 - 32)$
32

2. $s = 15 + 17 + 12$
$s = 12 + 15 + 17$
44

3. $m = 3 \times (\$1.25 + \$2.00)$
$m = (3 \times \$1.25) + (3 \times \$2.00)$
$\$9.75$

Lesson 3.3, page 44

1. $s = \frac{3}{4} \times (37 \times \$20)$; $\$185$; $\$555$
2. $s = (6 \times 2) \times \$5$; $\$60$
3. $m = 4 \times (\$8 + \$5)$; $m = (4 \times \$8) + (4 \times \$5)$; $\$52$
4. $p = 43 - (0.17p - 3)$
5. $t = [\$45 + (\$45 \times 0.2)] \div 2$; $\$27$

Lesson 3.4, page 45

1. $1.5 \times n = 90$; 60; 30
2. $(2 \times n) - \frac{3}{4} = 5\frac{1}{4}$; 3 miles; $2\frac{1}{4}$ miles
3. $(2 \times n) + \$12 = \$98$; $\$43$; $\$55$

Lesson 3.4, page 46

1. $60 \times p = \$17,880$; $\$298$
2. $\$1.55 = (3 \times \$0.25) + (d \times \$0.10)$; 8
3. $\$150 = m + (\$5 \times 8) + \$50$; $\$60$
4. $[23 - (2 \times 7)] \div 3 = f$; 3
5. $r = 792 - 5[(15 \times 5) + (25 \times 2)]$; 167

Lesson 3.4, page 47

1. $\$1.75 \times p = \$8.75$; 5
2. $\$8.50 \times h = \$170$; 20
3. $(4 \times \$5) + (4 \times c) = \$28$; $\$2$
4. $20 = 6.25 + 6.5 + h$; 7.25
5. $\$38.50 = (2 \times \$10.50) + (2 \times p)$; $\$8.75$

Lesson 3.5, page 48

1a. $m < -5$
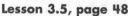

1b. $v \leq -3$
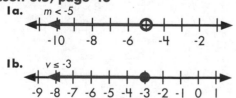

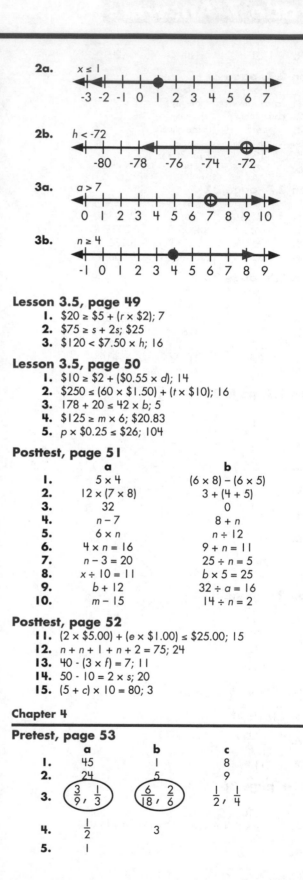

2a. $x \leq 1$

2b. $h < -72$

3a. $a > 7$

3b. $n \geq 4$

Lesson 3.5, page 49

1. $\$20 \geq \$5 + (r \times \$2)$; 7
2. $\$75 \geq s + 2s$; $\$25$
3. $\$120 < \$7.50 \times h$; 16

Lesson 3.5, page 50

1. $\$10 \geq \$2 + (\$0.55 \times d)$; 14
2. $\$250 \leq (60 \times \$1.50) + (t \times \$10)$; 16
3. $178 + 20 \leq 42 \times b$; 5
4. $\$125 \geq m \times 6$; $\$20.83$
5. $p \times \$0.25 \leq \$26$; 104

Posttest, page 51

	a	b
1.	5×4	$(6 \times 8) - (6 \times 5)$
2.	$12 \times (7 \times 8)$	$3 + (4 + 5)$
3.	32	0
4.	$n - 7$	$8 + n$
5.	$6 \times n$	$n \div 12$
6.	$4 \times n = 16$	$9 + n = 11$
7.	$n - 3 = 20$	$25 \div n = 5$
8.	$x \div 10 = 11$	$b \times 5 = 25$
9.	$b + 12$	$32 \div a = 16$
10.	$m - 15$	$14 \div n = 2$

Posttest, page 52

11. $(2 \times \$5.00) + (e \times \$1.00) \leq \$25.00$; 15
12. $n + n + 1 + n + 2 = 75$; 24
13. $40 - (3 \times f) = 7$; 11
14. $50 - 10 = 2 \times s$; 20
15. $(5 + c) \times 10 = 80$; 3

Chapter 4

Pretest, page 53

	a	b	c
1.	45	1	8
2.	24	5	9
3.	$\boxed{\frac{3}{9}, \frac{1}{3}}$	$\boxed{\frac{6}{18}, \frac{2}{6}}$	$\frac{1}{2}, \frac{1}{4}$
4.	$\frac{1}{2}$	3	
5.	1		

Grade 7 Answers

Pretest, page 54
6. 160
7. 105
8. 35
9. $37.40
10. $54.34 = r × 1.045; $52
11. $\frac{5}{24\frac{1}{2}} = \frac{e}{1}$; $\frac{8}{32\frac{1}{3}} = \frac{d}{1}$; Dez

Lesson 4.1, page 55
1. $\frac{\$8}{2\frac{1}{2}} = \frac{c}{1}$; $3.20
2. $\frac{4\frac{1}{2}}{7} = \frac{c}{1}$; $\frac{9}{14}$
3. $\frac{6\frac{1}{4}}{5} = \frac{f}{1}$; $1\frac{1}{4}$

Lesson 4.1, page 56
1. $\frac{3}{27\frac{1}{2}} = \frac{c}{1}$; $\frac{6}{53\frac{1}{2}} = \frac{m}{1}$; Melanie
2. $\frac{3\frac{1}{2}}{10\frac{1}{2}} = \frac{b}{1}$; $\frac{2\frac{1}{2}}{6\frac{1}{4}} = \frac{s}{1}$; Bob
3. $\frac{675}{2\frac{1}{2}} = \frac{t}{1}$; $\frac{1035}{3\frac{1}{4}} = \frac{m}{1}$; Marvin

Lesson 4.2, page 57

	a	b
1.	yes	no

Lesson 4.2, page 58

	a	b	c
1.	⟨$\frac{1}{3}$, $\frac{2}{6}$⟩	$\frac{3}{8}$, $\frac{1}{4}$	⟨$\frac{3}{5}$, $\frac{9}{15}$⟩
2.	⟨$\frac{3}{4}$, $\frac{9}{12}$⟩	$\frac{1}{2}$, $\frac{4}{8}$	⟨$\frac{5}{6}$, $\frac{15}{18}$⟩
3.	$\frac{5}{8}$, $\frac{4}{7}$	$\frac{1}{2}$, $\frac{1}{4}$	⟨$\frac{4}{3}$, $\frac{16}{12}$⟩
4.	⟨$\frac{6}{18}$, $\frac{2}{6}$⟩	⟨$\frac{3}{25}$, $\frac{6}{50}$⟩	$\frac{1}{8}$, $\frac{2}{10}$
5.	$\frac{1}{4}$, $\frac{2}{4}$	⟨$\frac{5}{10}$, $\frac{3}{6}$⟩	⟨$\frac{4}{24}$, $\frac{1}{4}$⟩
6.	$\frac{3}{5}$, $\frac{5}{3}$	⟨$\frac{7}{8}$, $\frac{21}{24}$⟩	$\frac{8}{23}$, $\frac{9}{46}$
7.	⟨$\frac{7}{4}$, $\frac{28}{16}$⟩	⟨$\frac{3}{9}$, $\frac{1}{3}$⟩	$\frac{16}{20}$, $\frac{9}{10}$
8.	$\frac{8}{100}$, $\frac{80}{50}$	$\frac{8}{12}$, $\frac{10}{14}$	⟨$\frac{15}{20}$, $\frac{3}{4}$⟩
9.	$\frac{9}{2}$, $\frac{12}{4}$	⟨$\frac{6}{3}$, $\frac{8}{4}$⟩	⟨$\frac{1}{3}$, $\frac{11}{33}$⟩
10.	⟨$\frac{12}{7}$, $\frac{36}{21}$⟩	$\frac{10}{12}$, $\frac{15}{20}$	$\frac{3}{4}$, $\frac{9}{16}$

Lesson 4.2, page 59

	a	b	c
1.	⟨$\frac{4}{3} = \frac{6}{4}$⟩	⟨$\frac{1}{4} = \frac{3}{12}$⟩	⟨$\frac{4}{5} = \frac{16}{20}$⟩
2.	⟨$\frac{8}{12} = \frac{2}{3}$⟩	⟨$\frac{30}{25} = \frac{6}{5}$⟩	$\frac{7}{3} = \frac{5}{2}$
3.	$\frac{9}{1} = \frac{18}{3}$	⟨$\frac{15}{4} = \frac{45}{12}$⟩	$\frac{2}{5} = \frac{4}{12}$

4.	⟨$\frac{7}{4} = \frac{21}{12}$⟩	$\frac{9}{2} = \frac{18}{6}$	⟨$\frac{5}{6} = \frac{15}{18}$⟩
5.	$\frac{5}{9} = \frac{10}{19}$	⟨$\frac{4}{3} = \frac{16}{12}$⟩	$\frac{7}{4} = \frac{14}{10}$
6.	⟨$\frac{12}{8} = \frac{18}{12}$⟩	⟨$\frac{14}{7} = \frac{6}{3}$⟩	$\frac{1}{5} = \frac{3}{16}$
7.	$\frac{1}{2} = \frac{6}{2}$	$\frac{8}{6} = \frac{12}{8}$	⟨$\frac{5}{4} = \frac{10}{8}$⟩
8.	⟨$\frac{2}{5} = \frac{6}{15}$⟩	$\frac{14}{6} = \frac{21}{8}$	$\frac{4}{5} = \frac{10}{16}$
9.	$\frac{3}{5} = \frac{9}{20}$	⟨$\frac{1}{3} = \frac{4}{12}$⟩	⟨$\frac{9}{6} = \frac{12}{8}$⟩
10.	⟨$\frac{7}{5} = \frac{28}{20}$⟩	$\frac{5}{4} = \frac{25}{16}$	$\frac{10}{13} = \frac{30}{26}$
11.	$\frac{4}{5} = \frac{20}{22}$	$\frac{1}{5} = \frac{3}{18}$	⟨$\frac{6}{7} = \frac{78}{91}$⟩
12.	⟨$\frac{2}{9} = \frac{30}{135}$⟩	⟨$\frac{8}{3} = \frac{96}{36}$⟩	$\frac{5}{2} = \frac{75}{20}$

Lesson 4.3, page 60

	a	b
1.	$1\frac{1}{2}$	5
2.	2	$1\frac{2}{3}$
3.	$\frac{1}{2}$	$\frac{1}{5}$

Lesson 4.3, page 61

	a	b
1.	2	$\frac{2}{3}$
2.	$\frac{1}{5}$	$\frac{4}{5}$
3.	$\frac{1}{6}$	2
4.	$\frac{1}{4}$	$\frac{3}{4}$

Lesson 4.4, page 62
1. $y = \frac{3}{2} \times 10$
2. $y = \frac{14}{11} \times 16$
3. $y = \frac{4}{145} \times 400$
4. $y = \frac{29}{5} \times 30$

Lesson 4.4, page 63
1. $x = \frac{1}{8} \times 80$
2. $x = \frac{1}{4} \times 100$
3. $x = \frac{2}{5} \times 8$
4. $x = \frac{21}{4} \times 6$
5. $x = \frac{1}{6} \times 36$

Lesson 4.5, page 64

	a	b
1.	$\frac{2}{3}$	$\frac{1}{3}$

Grade 7 Answers

2. $-\frac{1}{9}$ $-\frac{3}{2}$

Lesson 4.5, page 65

	a	b
1.	$\frac{8}{5}$	$\frac{1}{4}$
2.	$-\frac{1}{2}$	$-\frac{2}{9}$
3.	$-\frac{1}{3}$	$\frac{3}{2}$

Lesson 4.6, page 66

1. $4.84
2. $4.95; $94.95
3. 7
4. 36
5. 10; 69

Lesson 4.6, page 67

1. $45.00
2. $26.00
3. $2.08
4. $147.00; $747.00
5. $51.75
6. $4,462.50; $19,462.50

Posttest, page 68

	a	b	c
1.	9	2	24
2.	4	25	112
3.	$\left(\frac{15}{20}, \frac{3}{4}\right)$	$\frac{8}{12}, \frac{10}{14}$	$\left(\frac{4}{3}, \frac{16}{12}\right)$
4.	$\frac{1}{5}$	$\frac{1}{5}$	
5.	$-1\frac{1}{3}$		

Posttest, page 69

6. 30
7. $16\frac{1}{3}$
8. $\frac{10}{5} = \frac{x}{10}$; 20
9. $59.40; $719.40
10. $19.50; $1,219.50
11. $\frac{$108}{9} = \frac{x}{40}$; $480
12. $\frac{452}{2\frac{1}{4}} = \frac{a}{1}$; $\frac{1045}{3\frac{1}{2}} = \frac{b}{1}$; Bobbi

Mid Test, page 70

	a	b	c	d
1.	1	$1\frac{5}{12}$	$7\frac{11}{12}$	$4\frac{1}{2}$
2.	$\frac{1}{4}$	$\frac{1}{6}$	$3\frac{1}{12}$	$2\frac{2}{3}$
3.	$\frac{5}{24}$	$\frac{1}{4}$	$1\frac{13}{63}$	$\frac{3}{80}$
4.	$1\frac{1}{6}$	$4\frac{1}{5}$	$5\frac{1}{3}$	$2\frac{10}{27}$
5.	-5	-17	6	15
6.	7	-36	-47	-20
7.	-6	-7	17	-6
8.	7	-3	11	-12

Mid Test, page 71

	a	b	c	d
9.	-24	8	-30	60
10.	-7	-2	-6	4
11.	0.6	0.14	$0.\overline{009}$	
12.	5	-46	3	32
13.	no	yes	yes	no
14.	yes	yes	yes	no
15.	identity	associative	commutative	

Mid Test, page 72

	a	b
16.	$\frac{3}{4}$	$\frac{2}{7}$
17.	4	$\frac{3}{2}$ or $1\frac{1}{2}$
18.	$6 \times n > 12$	$3 \times (-4)$
19.	$2 + (45 \div 9)$	$4 - 9$
20.	$j < -72$	$k \le 4$

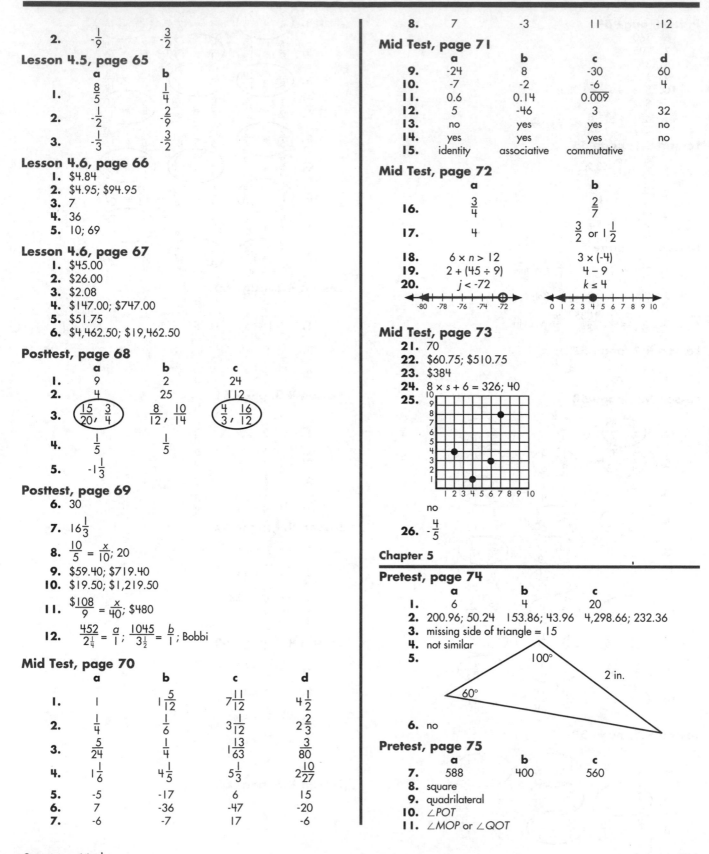

Mid Test, page 73

21. 70
22. $60.75; $510.75
23. $384
24. $8 \times s + 6 = 326$; 40
25.

no

26. $-\frac{4}{5}$

Chapter 5

Pretest, page 74

	a	b	c
1.	6	4	20
2.	200.96; 50.24	153.86; 43.96	4,298.66; 232.36

3. missing side of triangle = 15
4. not similar
5.
6. no

Pretest, page 75

	a	b	c
7.	588	400	560

8. square
9. quadrilateral
10. $\angle POT$
11. $\angle MOP$ or $\angle QOT$

12. 12
13. 150
14. 561

Lesson 5.1, page 76

1. $\frac{24}{36} = \frac{2}{3}$; $\frac{28}{42} = \frac{2}{3}$; $\frac{36}{54} = \frac{2}{3}$; similar

2. $\frac{18}{12} = \frac{3}{2}$; $\frac{12}{8} = \frac{3}{2}$; $\frac{12}{10} = \frac{6}{5}$; not similar

3. $\frac{30}{40} = \frac{3}{4}$; $\frac{27}{36} = \frac{3}{4}$; $\frac{24}{32} = \frac{3}{4}$; similar

Lesson 5.1, page 77

	a	b
1.	21 ft.	10 m
2.	24 m	25 in.
3.	15 cm	10 ft.

Lesson 5.1, page 78

1a. $\frac{AB}{XY} = \frac{BC}{YZ}$ $\frac{1}{2} = \frac{1}{2}$ similar

1b. $\frac{AB}{WX} = \frac{BC}{XY}$ $\frac{2.3}{1.5} \neq \frac{1.5}{1}$ not similar

2a. $\frac{AB}{TU} = \frac{BC}{UV} = \frac{CD}{VW} = \frac{DE}{WX} = \frac{EA}{XT}$
$\frac{2}{3} = \frac{2}{3} \neq \frac{1}{2} \neq \frac{1}{1} \neq \frac{1}{2}$ not similar

2b. $\frac{AB}{WX} = \frac{BC}{XY} = \frac{CD}{YZ} = \frac{DA}{ZW}$
$\frac{6}{3} = \frac{12}{6} = \frac{10}{5} = \frac{5}{2.5}$ similar

Lesson 5.2, page 79

1. 440
2. 8
3. 32
4. 36

Lesson 5.2, page 80

1. 54 feet
2. 80 feet
3. 17 inches
4. 27 miles
5. 1 inch = 7 feet
6. 1 inch = $\frac{4}{5}$ foot

Lesson 5.3, page 81
Use a protractor and ruler to check the accuracy of the drawings.

Lesson 5.3, page 82
Answers may vary. Use a protractor and ruler to check the accuracy of the drawings.

Lesson 5.3, page 83

	a	b	c
1.	no	yes	yes
2.	no	no	yes
3.	yes	yes	no
4.	no	yes	yes

Lesson 5.4, page 84

	a	b
1.	square or rectangle	rectangle
2.	quadrilateral	rectangle
3.	square	square

Lesson 5.4, page 85

	a	b
1.	triangle	trapezoid
2.	trapezoid	triangle
3.	triangle	triangle

Lesson 5.5, page 86

	a	b	c
1.	1.5 ft.	0.75 ft.	
2.		1.75 m	10.99 m
3.	6.5 in.		20.41 in.
4.	8.5 yd.	4.25 yd.	
5.		3.75 cm	23.55 cm
6.	30 in.		94.2 in.
7.	2.5 m	1.25 m	
8.		2.5 km	15.7 km
9.	10 ft.	5 ft.	
10.	90 cm		282.6 cm
11.		2 yd.	12.56 yd.
12.	3 mi.	1.5 mi.	

Lesson 5.5, page 87

	a	b	c
1.		4	12.56
2.	9		56.52
3.	4.6		28.89
4.		11	34.54
5.		24.4	76.62
6.	2.5		15.7
7.		34	106.76
8.		7	21.98
9.	6.5		40.82
10.	1.9		11.93
11.		6	18.84
12.	3.5		21.98
13.	2		12.56
14.		9	28.26
15.		11.2	35.17

Lesson 5.5, page 88

	a	b	c
1.	18.84 m	15.7 cm	46.47 in.
2.	1.57 km	69.08 ft.	32.03 m
3.	144.44 yd.	20.41 cm	131.88 mm
4.	13.50 cm	81.64 cm	125.6 in.
5.	3.93 cm	219.8 yd.	2.20 m
6.	0.06 mi.	6.28 yd.	79.25 m

Lesson 5.6, page 89

	a	b	c
1.	50.2 sq. ft.	113 sq. m	530.7 sq. cm
2.	1,017.4 sq. yd.	452.2 sq. km	153.9 sq. in.
3.	6 in.		28.3 sq. in.
4.		9 ft.	254.3 sq. ft.
5.		8.5 m	226.9 sq. m
6.	64 cm		3,215.4 sq. cm

Lesson 5.6, page 90

	a	b	c
1.		8	50.24
2.	6		113.04
3.		3	7.07
4.		22	379.94

Grade 7 Answers

5.	0.4		0.50
6.		180	25,434
7.		10	78.5
8.	4.5		63.59
9.	4.1		52.78
10.	5.5		94.99
11.		6	28.26
12.		24	452.16
13.	14		615.44
14.		18	254.34
15.	11		379.94

Lesson 5.6, page 91

	a	b	c
1.	197.46 m²	21.23 cm²	60.79 in.²
2.	19.63 km²	3.80 ft.²	706.5 m²
3.	32.15 yd.²	15.90 cm²	1,319.59 mm²
4.	8.76 m²	28.26 cm²	100.24 in.²
5.	10.63 cm²	452.16 yd.²	10.75 m²
6.	0.03 mi.²	1,533.61 yd.²	0.05 m²

Lesson 5.7, page 92

1. vertical
2. supplementary
3. supplementary
4. vertical
5. vertical
6. supplementary
7. 72°
8. 68°
9. 37°
10. 60°

Lesson 5.7, page 93

1. ∠GHJ or ∠GHM
2. ∠FHG
3. ∠JMK or ∠IMH
4. $\overline{ML}$
5. ∠IMH
6. ∠IMJ or ∠KMH
7. ∠CFD
8. ∠GFE
9. ∠AFC or ∠DFG
10. ∠CFE or ∠GFB
11. 77°
12. 68°
13. 52°; 104°
14. 79°; 158°

Lesson 5.7, page 94

1. ∠FBE/∠EBD, ∠GIH, HIJ
2. Answers will vary but may include ∠ABC/∠CBE, ∠CBD/∠DBF, ∠CBE/∠EBF, ∠EBF/∠FBA, ∠FBA/∠ABC, ∠LIK/∠LIH, ∠LIK/∠KIJ, ∠LIG/∠GIJ, ∠LIH/∠HIJ, ∠HIJ/∠JIK
3. ∠ABC/∠FBE, ∠CBE/∠FBA, ∠KIL/∠HIJ, ∠LIH/∠KIJ
4. Answers will vary but may include H.
5. Answers will vary.
6. 51°
7. 135°
8. 135°
9. 41°

10. 59°

Lesson 5.8, page 95

1. 145°
2. 75°
3. 35°
4. 110°
5. 98°
6. 58°

Lesson 5.9, page 96

	a	b	c
1.	54	84	56.25
2.	15	6	135
3.	165	12.5	11

Lesson 5.10, page 97

	a	b	c
1.	210	14	199.5
2.	270	162	272
3.	348	230	312.5

Lesson 5.11, page 98

	a	b	c
1.	2,340	3,600	968
2.	300	324	1,728
3.	1,056	648	375

Lesson 5.12, page 99

	a	b	c
1.	256	825	168.75
2.	546.88	1,296	400
3.	122.5	0.72	11,200

Lesson 5.13, page 100

1. 3
2. $1,383.75
3. $189
4. 437.5
5. 50.24

Lesson 5.13, page 101

1. 1
2. 51
3. 15,360
4. 42
5. $3\frac{1}{8}$
6. 400

Lesson 5.13, page 102

1. 336
2. 10,000
3. 432
4. $42.00
5. 750
6. 0.025

Posttest, page 103

	a	b	c
1.	6	12	75
2.	530.66; 81.64	254.34; 56.52	38.47; 21.98

3. missing side of triangle = 10
4. similar

Grade 7 Answers

5.
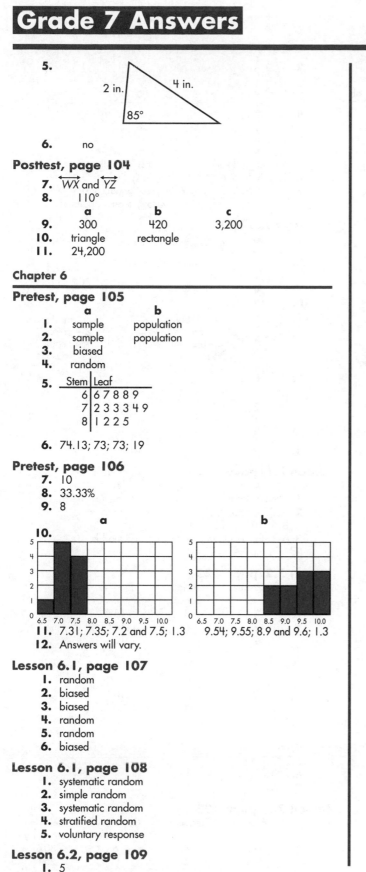
2 in.   4 in.   85°

6.   no

Posttest, page 104
7. $\overleftrightarrow{WX}$ and $\overleftrightarrow{YZ}$
8.   110°

	a	b	c
9.	300	420	3,200
10.	triangle	rectangle	

11.   24,200

Chapter 6

Pretest, page 105

	a	b
1.	sample	population
2.	sample	population
3.	biased	
4.	random	

5.
Stem	Leaf
6	6 7 8 8 9
7	2 3 3 3 4 9
8	1 2 2 5

6. 74.13; 73; 73; 19

Pretest, page 106
7. 10
8. 33.33%
9. 8

10.
a   b

11. 7.31; 7.35; 7.2 and 7.5; 1.3   9.54; 9.55; 8.9 and 9.6; 1.3
12. Answers will vary.

Lesson 6.1, page 107
1. random
2. biased
3. biased
4. random
5. random
6. biased

Lesson 6.1, page 108
1. systematic random
2. simple random
3. systematic random
4. stratified random
5. voluntary response

Lesson 6.2, page 109
1. 5

2. 16.67%
3. 20 or 21
4. 26.67%
5. 33 or 34
6. 20

Lesson 6.2, page 110
1. 20%
2. 36
3. 108
4. 9
5. 30%
6. 9

Lesson 6.2, page 111
1. 20
2. 100
3. 25%
4. 25
5. 35
6. 40

Lesson 6.3, page 112

	a	b
1.	8	37.1
	9	42.15
	9	23.1
	10	33.6
2.	174.6	516.9
	171	546.25
	171	349
	92	715

Lesson 6.4, page 113
1. The calorie range is much wider for restaurant 1 (500 as compared to 180). The mean calories are higher for restaurant 1 than they are for restaurant 2. The inference is that restaurant 2 is generally healthier.
2. The range of scores is smaller in class 2 than it is in class one. The mean score in class 2 is about 7 points higher than the mean score in class 1. It appears that the students in class 2 were better prepared for the test.
3. The range is higher by $1 for store # 1. However, the mean is about $1.10 lower. The inference is that both stores offer clothes of similar value.

Lesson 6.4, page 114
1. The range for the number of words in a sample of 8th grade pages is larger than the range of the number of words in a sample of 5th grade pages. There is about a 20-word difference between their means. There is little difference between the number of words on a page between 5th and 8th grade books.
2. The range of scores is larger for family 2 than for family 1. In addition, the mean donation of family 2 is about double the mean donation from family 1. Family 2 consistently donated more money to charity than family 1.
3. Both data sets have a small range. However, when looking at the distribution on the same scale, family size in New York City leans heavily toward small families while family size throughout the United States is more evenly spread across the scale.
4. The mean of Homeroom A is 6 books, and the mean of

Grade 7 Answers

Homeroom B is 7 books. Therefore, Homeroom B read on average more books than Homeroom A.

5. Both farms average the same amount of eggs over the course of the entire year.

Lesson 6.5, page 115

1. The mean growth for plants that were given light for 4 hours was 4.6 inches, while the mean growth for plants that were given light for 10 hours was 9.4 inches. Therefore, plants that are given more light grow more successfully.

2. The mean battery life for tablets playing videos was 5.7 hours. The mean battery life for tablets playing games was 7.54. Overall, tablets playing games lasted almost two hours longer than tablets playing videos.

Lesson 6.5, page 116

1. It appears the students 70 inches or taller travel on average 18 inches farther in the long jump than students who are less than 70 inches tall.

2. The inference is students who study between 1 and 3 hours per night scored on average about 10 points higher than students who study less than an hour each night.

3. It appears that there is no correlation between the amount of bait brought and the amount of fish caught. The fishermen who brought less than 50 pounds of bait caught on average 0.6 more fish than those who brought 50 pounds or more.

Posttest, page 117

1.

Stem	Leaf
9	1 2 3 6 7 7 8
10	1 3 4 5 8
11	1 2 5

2. 101.5; 101; 97; 24
3. 8
4. 40
5. 3
6. 20%
7. biased
8. random

Posttest, page 118

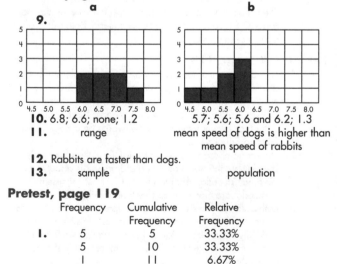

9. a b

10. 6.8; 6.6; none; 1.2   5.7; 5.6; 5.6 and 6.2; 1.3

11. range   mean speed of dogs is higher than mean speed of rabbits

12. Rabbits are faster than dogs.
13. sample   population

Pretest, page 119

	Frequency	Cumulative Frequency	Relative Frequency
1.	5	5	33.33%
	5	10	33.33%
	1	11	6.67%
	4	15	26.67%

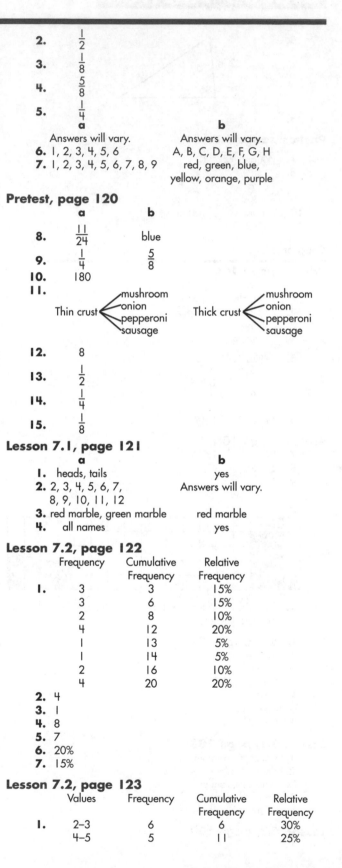

2. $\frac{1}{2}$

3. $\frac{1}{8}$

4. $\frac{5}{8}$

5. $\frac{1}{4}$

a	b
Answers will vary.	Answers will vary.
6. 1, 2, 3, 4, 5, 6	A, B, C, D, E, F, G, H
7. 1, 2, 3, 4, 5, 6, 7, 8, 9	red, green, blue, yellow, orange, purple

Pretest, page 120

	a	b
8.	$\frac{11}{24}$	blue
9.	$\frac{1}{4}$	$\frac{5}{8}$
10.	180	

11.

Thin crust — mushroom, onion, pepperoni, sausage   Thick crust — mushroom, onion, pepperoni, sausage

12. 8
13. $\frac{1}{2}$
14. $\frac{1}{4}$
15. $\frac{1}{8}$

Lesson 7.1, page 121

	a	b
1.	heads, tails	yes
2.	2, 3, 4, 5, 6, 7, 8, 9, 10, 11, 12	Answers will vary.
3.	red marble, green marble	red marble
4.	all names	yes

Lesson 7.2, page 122

	Frequency	Cumulative Frequency	Relative Frequency
1.	3	3	15%
	3	6	15%
	2	8	10%
	4	12	20%
	1	13	5%
	1	14	5%
	2	16	10%
	4	20	20%

2. 4
3. 1
4. 8
5. 7
6. 20%
7. 15%

Lesson 7.2, page 123

	Values	Frequency	Cumulative Frequency	Relative Frequency
1.	2–3	6	6	30%
	4–5	5	11	25%

Grade 7 Answers

	6–7	6	17	30%
	8–9	3	20	15%
2.	20–21	2	2	25%
	22–23	2	4	25%
	24–25	3	7	37.5%
	26–27	1	8	12.5%
3.	2–3	1	1	7.69%
	4–5	4	5	30.77%
	6–7	4	9	30.77%
	8–9	4	13	30.77%

Lesson 7.3, page 124

1. $\frac{3}{10}, \frac{4}{5}, \frac{7}{10}$ 5. $\frac{1}{3}$

2. $\frac{1}{6}$ 6. $\frac{5}{6}$

3. $\frac{1}{2}$ 7. $\frac{2}{3}$

4. $\frac{1}{3}$

Lesson 7.3, page 125

1. $\frac{3}{10}$ 5. $\frac{1}{2}$ 9. $\frac{1}{6}$

2. $\frac{2}{5}$ 6. $\frac{1}{3}$ 10. $\frac{1}{3}$

3. $\frac{1}{5}$ 7. $\frac{1}{6}$

4. $\frac{1}{10}$ 8. $\frac{1}{6}$

Lesson 7.3, page 126

1. $\frac{1}{2}$ 6. $\frac{1}{6}$ 11. $\frac{1}{3}$

2. $\frac{3}{10}$ 7. $\frac{1}{6}$ 12. $\frac{1}{6}$

3. $\frac{1}{5}$ 8. $\frac{5}{12}$ 13. $\frac{5}{12}$

4. $\frac{7}{10}$ 9. $\frac{1}{3}$ 14. $\frac{1}{3}$

5. $\frac{1}{3}$ 10. $\frac{1}{3}$ 15. $\frac{1}{4}$

Lesson 7.4, page 127

	a	b
1.	yes	no
2.	yes	no
3.	no	yes
4.	no	no
5.	no	no
6.	yes	yes

Lesson 7.4, page 128

1. Spinner must have an equal number of same size spaces with an equal number of stars and diamonds.
2. Spinner must have an equal number of same size spaces with numbers 1, 2, 3, and 4.
3.
4. Answers will vary but may include

Lesson 7.5, page 129

	a	b
1.	not equal	equal
2.	equal	not equal
3.	equal	equal
4.	not equal	not equal

Lesson 7.5, page 130

1.   2.

3.   4.

Lesson 7.5, page 131

1a. $\frac{2}{6}$ or $\frac{1}{3}$ 1b. $\frac{3}{6}$ or $\frac{1}{2}$

2a. $\frac{1}{2}$ 2b. $\frac{1}{2}$

3a. $\frac{11}{90}$ 3b. $\frac{10}{85}$ or $\frac{2}{17}$

3c. the first bag

4a. $\frac{1}{36}$ 4b. $\frac{2}{36}$

4c. $\frac{3}{36}$ 4d. $\frac{4}{36}$

4e. $\frac{5}{36}$ 4f. $\frac{6}{36}$

4g. $\frac{5}{36}$ 4h. $\frac{4}{36}$

4i. $\frac{3}{36}$ 4j. $\frac{2}{36}$

4k. $\frac{1}{36}$

5a. $\frac{16}{25}$ 5b. $\frac{12}{19}$

Lesson 7.6, page 132

	a	b
1.	36	12
2.	8	104
3.	36	72
4.	208	144

Lesson 7.6, page 133

1. 288   2. 60   3. 320   4. 20   5. 180   6. 192   7. 280

Lesson 7.7, page 134

1. 12

2. 16

Lesson 7.7, page 135

1. 8
2. 18
3. 6;

Grade 7 Answers

Lesson 7.7, page 136

1.

	black	brown	blue	khaki
black	bl/bl	bl/br	bl/blu	bl/k
blue	blu/bl	blu/br	blu/blu	blu/k
red	r/bl	r/bl	r/bl	r/k
green	g/bl	g/br	g/blu	g/k
yellow	y/bl	y/br	y/blu	y/k

$\frac{2}{20}$ or $\frac{1}{10}$

2.

	1	2	3	4	5	6	7	8
1	2	3	4	5	6	7	8	9
2	3	4	5	6	7	8	9	10
3	4	5	6	7	8	9	10	11
4	5	6	7	8	9	10	11	12
5	6	7	8	9	10	11	12	13
6	7	8	9	10	11	12	13	14

$\frac{5}{48}$

Lesson 7.8, page 137

Strategies will vary.

1. 8 **2.** 20 **3.** $\frac{1}{9}$ **4.** $\frac{1}{26}$

Lesson 7.8, page 138

Strategies will vary.

1. $\frac{1}{25}$ **2.** 48 **3.** 27 **4.** $\frac{1}{8}$

Lesson 7.8, page 139

Strategies will vary.

1. 36 **2.** $\frac{1}{6}$ **3.** $\frac{1}{9}$ **4.** 12

Posttest, page 140

1. 3 **2.** 4 **3.** 9 **4.** 8 **5.** 24 **6.** 11–15 **7.** $\frac{1}{3}$

8. Answers will vary depending on intervals chosen in column 1.

Cars	Frequency	Cumulative Frequency	Relative Frequency
91–95	3	3	20%
96–100	4	7	26.67%
101–105	4	11	26.67%
106–110	1	12	6.67%
111–115	3	15	20%

9. $\frac{1}{8}$ **10.** $\frac{1}{2}$ **11.** $\frac{1}{2}$ **12.** $\frac{3}{8}$

Posttest, page 141

13.

Racing < red, black, silver   Mountain < red, black, silver

14. 6 **15.** $\frac{1}{2}$ **16.** $\frac{1}{3}$ **17.** $\frac{1}{6}$

18. ●●●○○○ Answers may vary.

19. Answers will vary but may include 1, 1, 2, 2.

20. 3,150

Final Test, page 142

	a	b	c
1.	-4	$4\frac{11}{12}$	3
2.	4	-2	-5
3.	-3	1	-6
4.	$\frac{1}{2}$	-11	-1

5.	-69	360	108
6.	-355	-581	$\frac{1}{10}$
7.	6	-5	-19
8.	22	-6	-9
9.	0.6; T	0.14; T	0.008; T

Final Test, page 143

10. $(6 \times s) + 7 = 331$; 54

11. $100 = 30 + w$; 70

12. $\frac{3}{8}$; $\frac{3}{16}$; $\frac{13}{16}$

13. 3,750

14. $\frac{27}{25}$

15. 21.98

Final Test, page 144

	a	b	c	d
16.	yes	no	yes	yes
17.	$1.6\overline{6}$			
18.	29; 31.5; 30	24; 18; 25		
19.	50.24; 200.96	37.68; 113.04	113.04; 1,017.36	
20.	270	2.16	96	

Final Test, page 145

21. 145°

22. 35°

23. 145°

24. 35°

	a	b	c
25.	60	1,408	1,296

26.

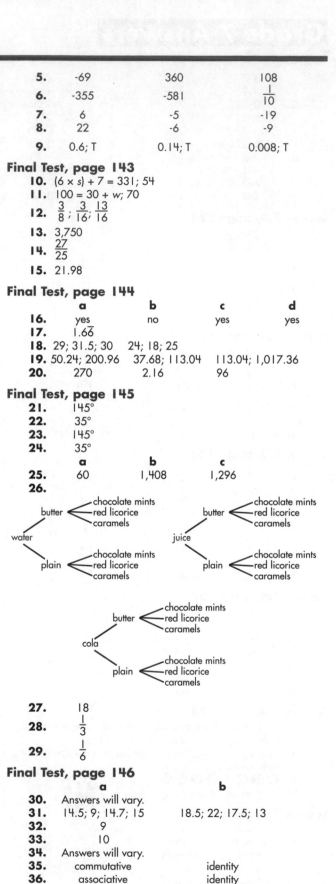

27. 18

28. $\frac{1}{3}$

29. $\frac{1}{6}$

Final Test, page 146

	a	b
30.	Answers will vary.	
31.	14.5; 9; 14.7; 15	18.5; 22; 17.5; 13
32.	9	
33.	10	
34.	Answers will vary.	
35.	commutative	identity
36.	associative	identity